FIDEL'S CUBA

a revolution in pictures

OSVALDO SALAS
ROBERTO SALAS
PHOTOGRAPHERS

FIDEL'S CUBA

A REVOLUTION IN PICTURES

JON LEE ANDERSON

foreword

GREGORY TOZIAN

writer

DOUG SMITH
TED ANDERSON

editors

THUNDER'S MOUTH PRESS
BEYOND WORDS PUBLISHING

co-publishers

Beyond Words Publishing, Inc.
20827 N.W. Cornell Road, Suite 500
Hillsboro, Oregon 97124-9808
503-531-8700
1-800-284-9673

Thunder's Mouth Press
841 Broadway, 4th floor
New York, NY 10003
212-614-7880

DESIGN AND TYPOGRAPHY: Principia Graphica
EDITORS: Doug Smith and Ted Anderson
PROOFREADER: Marvin Moore

Printed in Hong Kong
Distributed to the book trade by Publishers Group West
Gallery representation by Fahey/Klein Gallery, Los Angeles, California

Library of Congress Cataloging-in-Publication Data
Salas, Osvaldo, 1914–
    Fidel's Cuba : a revolution in pictures / photographs by Osvaldo
  and Roberto Salas ; text by Gregory Tozian ; edited by Ted Anderson
  and Doug Smith.
        p. cm.
    ISBN 1-56025-192-1
    1. Cuba—History—1933–1959—Pictorial works. 2. Cuba—History—
  Revolution, 1959—Pictorial works. 3. Cuba—History—1959—
  Pictorial works. 4. Castro, Fidel, 1927– —Pictorial works.
  5. Cuba—History. I. Salas, Roberto, 1940– . II. Tozian,
  Gregory. III. Anderson, Ted, 1942– . IV. Smith, Doug (Gordon
  Douglas). V. Title.
  F1788.S314 1998
  972.9106′4′0222—dc21   98-28731
                                                              CIP

THE CORPORATE MISSION OF BEYOND WORDS PUBLISHING, INC.:
Inspire to Integrity

*To my father, Osvaldo. If someone were to ask me what the one
thing that you had left me was, I'd have to say it was your
continual quest to improve your work. There is always a better
way. That's the thing that keeps me going. I know I have only
skimmed the top of your files and legacy. But how can I sum
up your life and dedication on a few sheets of photographic
paper? To put a mountain in a grain of salt? They will never
know what you left behind. I'm still trying to follow your foot-
steps and always use your example. Someone said an image
was more than a thousand words. Like you, I prefer a thousand images. I finally know and understand your philosophy.
You were always right: "Our best work and photographs are the
ones we will do tomorrow."*

ROBERTO SALAS
Havana, Cuba

*To my father, Marvin Anderson, lawyer, historian, theologian,
professor, dean, and chancellor, who taught me the love of
life, learning, adventure, and achievement, but most of all,
the love of family. Thanks, Pop.*

TED ANDERSON
Portland, Oregon

To my mentor, David Christy, who taught me to live my dreams.

DOUG SMITH
Palm Springs, California

*To the Salas photographic legacy. To my parents, George and
Verna Tozian. Thanks, as ever. Many thanks also to Heather
Joyner, Thane Tienson, Robert Goff, and Marvin Moore for their
invaluable assistance with the manuscript.*

GREGORY TOZIAN
Portland, Oregon

CONTENTS

f o r e w o r d

FEW LEADERS of the twentieth century have aroused such a widespread and enduring fascination as Cuba's Fidel Castro; rarely in modern times has a political event provoked such distinct passions as the revolution he led to power in 1959. The whole epic history of Fidel's Cuba is illustrated for us in this remarkable book of photographs taken by Osvaldo Salas and his son, Roberto. ▷ Here, we see Fidel Castro as a clean-shaven young lawyer, as a bearded guerrilla comandante, playing his favorite sport of baseball, giving emotional speeches, meeting Papa Hemingway, and conferring quietly with his revolutionary comrade Che Guevara. And we see also the faces of ordinary Cubans, themselves transformed into historic personalities through the Salases' lens. ▷ But the story of Osvaldo and Roberto Salas is almost as extraordinary as that of the revolution they documented. At the age of forty-four and eighteen, respectively, father and son returned to their homeland, cameras in hand, leaving behind their lives as émigrés in New York City. An immigrant's son, Osvaldo had lived there since his teens, while his son, Roberto, had been born in the Bronx. They knew only that with Fidel's rebel victory and the flight of dictator Batista, a new era had begun in Cuba, and that they, as Cubans, wanted to be a part of it. Neither realized that Fidel's revolution would become a life's work for each of them. ▷ Their photographs remind us that Fidel Castro has lived out his adult life in the public eye. Endowed with an acute sense of timing and occasion, Fidel has always displayed an awareness of the power of the graphic image and has encouraged the presence of photographers. As a result, most of the key moments of his life have been visually recorded. With his emotional, highly mobile face and the animated gestures of a man who is compelled to speak out loud—to argue, to persuade, to be center stage—Fidel is a photographer's dream. It is little wonder that the Salases became enthralled with their subject and stayed on, living out their lives, as have so many other Cubans, in an unusually intimate symbiosis with that of Cuba's *Jefe Máximo*. ▷ For a few short years, they also had the opportunity to photograph another extraordinary man: Ernesto "Che" Guevara, the gruff but charismatic Argentine revolutionary who was Fidel's closest confidante until he left Cuba to lead new revolutions elsewhere. With his long hair, pale skin, and piercing eyes that belied the intensity of his convictions, Che was incredibly photogenic but a difficult subject. He was moody, capable of playing to the camera one moment and resenting its intrusion the next. Blessed with the intuitive ability of some photographers to peer into a person's soul, both Salases realized that the best portraits of Che were those that caught him lost in thought. ▷ Perhaps Che's ambivalence with the camera came from the fact that he was a photography aficionado himself and fully understood the power of the medium. Before meeting Fidel Castro and joining his cause, Guevara had worked as an itinerant portrait photographer in Mexico City. It was a hobby he never gave up, and right through to the end of his life, Che habitually took snapshots of life around him. ▷ Moments before his execution in Bolivia in 1967, Che was photographed for the last time, by his enemies. It shows him captive but uncowed, glaring rebelliously back at the camera. Osvaldo Salas took a final, posthumous portrait of Che; it is an immensely powerful picture of a *picture*: Che's face on the night of the mass public wake held in his honor in Havana's Plaza de la Revolución. With the Cuban flag fluttering in the foreground, the photograph evokes the immensity of Che's revolutionary vision for the world, and the enormity of his loss for Cuba. ▷ There are photographs here that evoke Cuba's status as a flash point in the Cold War between East and West. The images of the Bay of Pigs invasion, of Soviet cosmonaut Yuri Gagarin, and of Leonid Brezhnev are testimonials to Cuba's acrid confrontation with the United States and alignment with the Soviet Union. Other photographs remind us that it wasn't always that way. Here we see Cuba's newly triumphant *barbudos* visiting the Lincoln Memorial and an early, happy visit by Fidel to the United Nations. Above all, what these pictures remind us today is that a Cold War still persists between Washington and Havana, a state of affairs as dated—and yet as *real*—as these photographs. ▷ This book appears as Americans are "rediscovering" Cuba. Attracted by the island's booming cultural scene, its beaches—and above all, its people—they are traveling there in increasingly large numbers. They are having to do so illegally, via third countries, because of the long-standing trade and travel restrictions imposed by Washington. Indeed, the embargo has been in place for so long that only older Americans and Cubans recall the time when they were able to travel back and forth with the easy familiarity of close neighbors. ▷ Today, things seem to be easing a little; maybe, one day soon, Americans and Cubans will again be able to visit one another's homes openly. In the meantime, it seems to me that these photographs—taken without acrimony by two men who have lived in both worlds—help to bridge the gap by putting history in its place. ▷ I had the good fortune of meeting Osvaldo Salas not long before he died. It was in 1992 in London, where he had come for an exhibition of his photos. *El viejo* Salas was an open, friendly man and a good storyteller who spoke in a disconcertingly accurate American English with the accent and colloquialisms of mid-century New York City. Later, in Cuba, I got to know Roberto, whom I found to have the same generous and friendly personality as his father, *and* the sharp wit of a streetwise New York boy—who just happens to be Cuban. ▷ In the end, if I have to sum up what I admire most about the Salases and their work, it is their professionalism. This book is a testament to that spirit and also to the lives they lived alongside one another, as father and son, each behind his own camera. And I know that Roberto continues working even now, recording the ongoing life of his country, portraying history as he sees it—in Fidel's Cuba.

Jon Lee Anderson

The force of human presence;

the poetry of stone, and coral,

the values of space,

are transcended and fixed

in Osvaldo Salas's masterful images.

ALEJO CARPENTIER

author of *The Lost Steps*

REVOLUTIONS are notoriously unpredictable. However, one thing they can be depended on to do is change a lot of people's lives—drastically and forever. The Cuban Revolution is certainly no exception. ▷ That now-legendary uprising reached critical mass around 2 A.M. on New Year's Day 1959, when U.S.-government- and mob-supported dictator Fulgencio Batista fled by plane from Havana to the Dominican Republic, taking with him a reported $300 million worth of ill-gotten gains. ▷ As guerrilla leader Fidel Castro rode triumphantly in his Roman-style military convoy across the island to nearly universal approval of Cuba's six million people, he was transformed from an ambitious young rebel/attorney into a dynamic and unbending world leader. Sugarcane cutters and cigar rollers, once acquiescent, became zealots for the cause of Cuban independence after nearly five hundred years of foreign rule. Illiterate farmers and domestic servants enrolled in new government literacy programs and became avid book and newspaper readers—although Castro carefully screened what they read. Hundreds of thousands of formerly well-to-do *Cubanos* turned into bitter exiles, longing for the day when they could return home from ninety miles away in South Florida and reclaim their confiscated properties. Least fortunate were the Batista soldiers and citizens charged with varying degrees of "war crimes." Thousands of Cubans became prisoners or were tried and executed. The Revolution was not bloodless. ▷ Two persons unlikely to be transformed by the Revolution were not in Cuba when Castro prevailed. Cuban émigré Osvaldo Salas and American-born Roberto Salas, father-and-son photographers living in New York City, listened to accounts of the Revolution on the radio. They dreamt of Cuba and of Castro, whom they had met and photographed in Manhattan four years earlier. ▷ Two days after Batista fled, eighteen-year-old Roberto Salas went to Idlewild Airport, bent on "going home." He discovered a Cuban government airplane waiting on the tarmac, grounded because of the chaotic events on the island. To his delight, he learned the plane would leave anyway, spiriting homeward a cargo of jubilant Cuban exile-patriots brazenly carrying guns, hand grenades, and other weapons. ▷ "I have no idea what they thought they were going to do with all that stuff when they got to Cuba," Roberto Salas remembers, "but I knew I was going with them." ▷ Armed with only his camera bag, Roberto arrived in Havana that night. A week later, at the personal invitation of Castro himself, Roberto's forty-four-year-old father, Osvaldo, came to Cuba with his cameras. ▷ Throughout the years that followed, as Cuba's swing toward communism made headlines, the former New Yorkers thoroughly tracked Castro and his exploits through their camera viewfinders. The thousands of Salas photographs that remain today are a testament to how well they did their jobs during such events as the tragic Bay of Pigs fiasco and a missile crisis that left the world teetering on the brink of nuclear war. As worldwide fellow travelers with Castro and as press photographers for the government's official daily news-paper, *Revolución*, the Salases documented with compelling style a pivotal period in twentieth-century history. ▷ The full story of how the Revolution changed the Salases from frustrated U.S. photographers scratching out lower-middle-class livings to important players in Cuba's period of *fotografía épica revolucionaria* is one of the more intriguing tales in modern photography.

OSVALDO SALAS FREIRE was born in Havana on March 29, 1914. From an early age, he had artistic leanings. When he was twelve, Osvaldo's working-class parents enrolled him in painting classes at the Academia de San Alenjandro in Havana. ▷ Shortly thereafter, the boy received a rude awakening when his railroad-mechanic father moved the family to New York in hopes of finding a better job. Tough times ensued, negating any chance for an immigrant son to further explore art. As the family became increasingly destitute, the fifteen-year-old Osvaldo was forced to drop out of school and labor as a mechanic's apprentice on the New Jersey Railroad. A string of welding jobs followed, ending one day in a factory accident that would plague him the rest of his life. Osvaldo severely injured his right ankle and was laid up for eight months. Upon recovery, he reluctantly went back to welding, at a bench that allowed him to stay off his weakened ankle. ▷ In 1947, Osvaldo, then thirty-three, found himself working as a bench welder for International Telephone and Telegraph (IT&T). By this time, he had a wife, Elsa, and two children, Roberto, born 1940, and Joann, born 1944. Osvaldo considered himself trapped in a dead-end job, without any opportunity to express himself artistically, and abandoned all hope of ever returning to Cuba. One day, however, a fellow employee came into Osvaldo's shop and asked him to spot-weld a defective metal tank for developing photographic film. Soon Osvaldo was making chemical trays and other darkroom paraphernalia for IT&T's amateur photographers. He began to take an interest in the devices he was assembling in his off-hours. ▷ On a lark, Osvaldo bought a $25 "Perfect" 35mm camera at a pawnshop and joined the Inwood Camera Club of New York. Shortly thereafter, he won a first place in the club's annual photo contest. His winning picture, a moody daytime study of a teeming street in Chinatown, was the first photograph in which Osvaldo took pride. His image of a cross hanging above a chow-mein-noodle factory and tattoo parlor with passersby reveals remarkably sophisticated composition for a beginner. Osvaldo's winning picture, its excellent tonal range highlighted by an illuminating slash of light, is also significant as a portrait of an immigrant community in Manhattan seen through the eyes of a man who felt himself to be very much a foreigner. With encouragement from his peers, Salas bought a 4" x 5" Speed Graphic camera, then the standard of newsmen and street photographers everywhere. By 1949, Salas had amassed other club prizes and was voted one of Inwood's top-ten photographers. ▷ With no formal training, Osvaldo Salas had found his creative medium. He became an aggressive amateur photographer. Friends and acquaintances could count on him to shoot almost anything: neighborhood birthday parties, bar mitzvahs, weddings, and even funerals. ▷ One evening, Osvaldo found himself hired to take pictures for a party at which welterweight boxing champion Kid Gavilan appeared. He photographed the fighter and, through a chain of coincidences, saw his portrait get impressive play in the Havana daily newspaper *Alerta*. (Ironically, that newspaper's offices would be taken over in

1959 by Castro's troops, becoming the first headquarters for the newspaper *Revolución*—which would employ Osvaldo and Roberto Salas.) ▷ "That was a hell of a time for my father," remembers Roberto Salas. "He'd be welding all day and working in the darkroom at home every night until 1 A.M. Every day he worked eighteen to twenty hours like that, and finally he had to ask himself, 'Am I a welder or a photographer?'" ▷ The success of the Kid Gavilan photo gave Osvaldo the confidence to become a photographer. In 1950, he took a risk and set up a small studio at 319 West 50th Street in Manhattan, across the street from the mecca of the fight game, Madison Square Garden. That same year, Osvaldo gave his ten-year-old son Roberto his first camera. ▷ "We had a wall painted white as a backdrop and a small platform," says Roberto. "We used three 500-watt tungsten lamps for lighting—one main [light], one fill, and one hair light. It was a cheap setup, but it worked." ▷ Osvaldo, dubbed "Charlie" Salas by the boxing community after a like-named fighter on the West Coast, became one of the main stringers for the most famous fight periodical of the day, *Ring* magazine. For every major bout, he and his son walked over to the Garden to take pictures, capturing on film such sportsmen as Floyd Patterson and Archie Moore, Roberto's favorite. His affable manner gained Osvaldo a reputation as an easy photogra-

Osvaldo Salas's first award-winning photograph. Chinatown, New York, 1959.

pher to pose for. *Ring*, in a feature on Osvaldo and his work in the late '50s, acknowledged that he even had the notoriously gruff Sugar Ray Robinson eating out of his hand. "I get anything I want out of Ray," Osvaldo told the magazine, "even if he hasn't come across with the free trip to Europe that he keeps promising me." ▷ Soon, the Cuban-émigré photographer had *Life* magazine courting him for rights to one of his most notable pictures. Osvaldo had been the only one to get a clear shot of a frightening split to Rocky Marciano's nose during a climactic fight. That photo marked the first time Osvaldo made the pages of a national general-interest magazine. ▷ The Salases' photographic skills also earned them permanent press passes to Yankee Stadium, the Polo Grounds, and Ebbets Field. They knew all the great baseball players of the '50s, and Osvaldo frequently took pictures of stars such as Jackie Robinson, Joe DiMaggio, Ted Williams, and Mickey Mantle. ▷ Thanks to the press credentials he shared with his father, Roberto had the chance to rub lenses with some of the legendary news photographers of his day—people like "Weegee" (Arthur Fellig, then in his fifties). "I first met Weegee taking pictures at the Ringling Brothers Circus," Salas says. "He'd gotten past his whole 'Naked City' phase he was famous for and was shooting experimental stuff. He chain-smoked these cheap White Owl cigars—when you looked in the back seat of his car there were boxes of them in there. Being Cuban, I told him he should smoke something better—Havanas. He wasn't interested." ▷ The proximity to Madison Square Garden brought Osvaldo into contact with a galaxy of motion-picture stars, artists, and musical celebrities.

Among those he photographed in striking black-and-white publicity portraits were Marilyn Monroe, Cary Grant, Humphrey Bogart, jazz trumpeter Louis Armstrong, and painter Salvador Dali. Osvaldo's assignments came regularly from a handful of influential Latin American newspapers and magazines, including *Alerta*, *El Clarín* (Buenos Aires), *Revista Deportiva* and *Nacional*

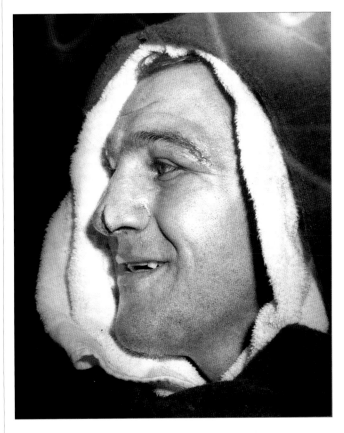

(Venezuela), and *Cinema Reporter* (Mexico). ▷ The people who posed for the Salases in the 1950s were rich and famous, the icons of their generation. Reality for Osvaldo and his son, however, was more modest: they languished at the other end of the economic scale. Osvaldo's published pictures netted a mere ten to fifteen dollars each. ▷ "If you're just an artist in New York and not a businessman,

Osvaldo Salas's picture of a career-threatening split to fighter Rocky Marciano's nose, his first photograph in Life *magazine, March 7, 1955, under the headline "Most Famous Nose in Sports."*

you're going to starve," Roberto Salas says. "And my father was no businessman. He never had a bank account. I collected on all his bills for him. My father was always against my becoming a photographer. He thought I should become an engineer. He didn't want me to work from sunup to sundown for peanuts like he did."

IN THE EISENHOWER ERA of 1950s New York, there was a photographic revolution going on, led by a small band of brave new shooters. Their critical lenses were aimed at disaffected social classes, racial inequities, and the random violence that went unphotographed by most American

picture-makers. Photographers such as Robert Frank, Lee Friedlander, and Diane Arbus led the way in documenting ennui and hopelessness with stark and painfully personal images. Although Osvaldo Salas himself felt strongly disenfranchised from the American Dream, he remained essentially unaffected by these new directions in photography. ▷ The pictures that Osvaldo took in New York during 1950–58 are clearly head and shoulders above the neighborhood-party and wedding photographs he'd started out making. Often staged, Osvaldo's flash-on-camera celebrity portraits are excellent examples of publicity work. Nevertheless, however interesting Osvaldo's photos of entertainers and sports figures are today, they do not convey the intimacy and energy that emanate from his Cuba-influenced work. ▷ Amidst his daily grind of freelance work, fate smiled on Osvaldo on October 30, 1955. That afternoon, a Cuban journalist friend dropped by the Salases' small West 50th Street studio with a well-bred and intense Cuban named Fidel Castro. Osvaldo instinctively started taking pictures. Castro, who barely stopped talking long enough to draw a breath, invited the photographer to

"Jolting Joe" DiMaggio, baseball great, at Yankee Stadium, 1954.

Osvaldo Salas with Cary Grant during interview/photo session for a Cuban magazine, New York, 1956. (Photo by Roberto Salas)

bring his camera that evening to the nearby Palm Garden, a popular dance and events hall. Upon arriving at the hall at the prescribed time that evening, Osvaldo was surprised to find his new Cuban acquaintance the star attraction. Castro, recently released after a two-year jail sentence for leading a disastrously bloody attack on a Cuban government army barracks, spoke passionately to a crowd of some eight hundred exiles that evening. He was raising funds for his budding revolutionary effort, which he called "the 26th of July Movement" in honor of the date of his ill-fated attack against Batista. Osvaldo, like many that evening, was immediately and forcefully impressed by Castro. Here, finally, was a subject suited to his creativity. Osvaldo photographed the fund-raising rally, selling the pictures of the revolutionary's New York visit to a regular client: the opposition-minded Cuban magazine *Bohemia*— then the largest-circulation periodical in all of Latin America. Over his brief stay in the city, Castro visited the photo studio yet again and convinced Osvaldo of the urgency of overthrowing Batista. Osvaldo's photographs from that week in 1955—of Castro's heartfelt speech, of the leader before a table laden with crumpled Yankee dollars, and of Castro strolling through Central Park in a double-breasted suit, cigar in hand—are notable examples of the high-quality portraiture he had worked so hard to perfect, combined with the on-the-spot news feel of good *reportage*. Newly inspired, Osvaldo continued to take pictures and raise money for "the Movement" whenever possible, as he did at a Cuban-exile rally in New York on July 26, 1956. One photograph from this event shows a

blonde woman with a drawn expression and accusatory stare carrying a sign reading "We are fighting against Batista. He is killing our sons, husbands, and parents." The subject of the picture was a member of the "female section" of the U.S. branch of the 26th of July Movement, an organization that Roberto Salas soon joined. Throughout his

life, Osvaldo Salas, although he never considered himself an official member of any political party, remained a fervent *fidelista*, or supporter of Fidel Castro's original liberation movement. "The first time he met Fidel, in '55, my father was political only in the sense that he thought a change was necessary in Cuba," Roberto Salas

Jazz trumpeter Louis Armstrong, New York, 1958.

says, looking back. "It wasn't a political thing, it was a patriotic thing. For a better life for other Cubans, we felt Batista was bad, Castro was better." ▷ During the 1957–58 school year, times for the Salases were tougher than usual. Roberto was forced to quit high school to work full time, as his father had done—a fact that saddened Osvaldo but delighted Roberto. ▷ "I never wanted to be anything but a photographer, anyway," Roberto Salas admits. "The people I admired in those days, the guys I most wanted to be like, were [photographers] Philippe Halsman, Richard Avedon, and [W.] Eugene Smith." ▷ Like his father, Roberto would get his chance to express himself fully in photography through participation in the 26th of July Movement. ▷ Following news from the homeland that the U.S. ambassador to Cuba had snubbed protests against the Batista regime, Roberto set out with a group of Cuban exiles to make a "visual statement" that could not be ignored by U.S. citizens. The young Salas and a few willing co-conspirators took their only 26th of July flag to the Statue of Liberty one morning and hung the standard from the crown of the monument. Roberto Salas's symbolic image of the Cuban liberation flag flying atop America's most famous symbol of freedom made a big splash in all the New York newspapers on August 3, 1957. *Life* magazine editors eagerly contacted the then-sixteen-year-old photographer, as they had his father, and his picture appeared in that magazine's pages. ▷ Roberto became so passionate about Cuba's liberation struggles that he spent much time trying to convince higher-ups in the Movement that he should be allowed to fight in the mountains with Castro's guerrillas.

They always told him he was too young. ▷ By the end of the 1950s, both Osvaldo and Roberto finally had strong patriotic feelings to associate with their work. The triumph of Castro's revolution as it moved down the mountains of the Sierra Maestra and swept across Cuba into Havana would also usher the Salases home.

PHOTOGRAPHY is all about light. But throughout Latin America and the Caribbean, conditions photographic—like those economic and social—have often seemed shadowed by North America. ▷ Although Cuba was at the forefront of photographic advancements among Latin American countries since the introduction of daguerreotypes in the 1840s, until Castro's revolution one hundred years later, Cuban photography lacked a unified movement. Under Castro, Cuban photography became a socially significant act—existing for the good of the state. Before that event, pictures of a socially significant nature were taken by foreign news correspondents in Cuba as often as they were by native documentarians and photojournalists. ▷ A few Cubans, like '30s photographer José Tabio, did sporadically

U.S. President Dwight D. Eisenhower throwing in the first pitch for the 1955 World Series game between the New York Yankees and Brooklyn Dodgers. Yankee manager Casey Stengle and Dodger manager Walter Alston look on.

break the mold and create groundbreaking images on social themes. Constantino Arias continued in a similar direction in the 1950s, although he alternated moving depictions of slum dwellers with glitzy assignments for the Cuban bourgeoisie. Similar part-time social *reportage* was practiced by Alberto Korda and Raúl Corrales, future fellow shooters of the Salases at *Revolución*. Korda, arguably the most famous photographer in 1950s Cuba, relied primarily on fashion assignments, though he also ventured into the streets to shoot images of poverty. Much of Corrales's work, when he wasn't shooting publicity photos, targeted the poor living conditions of farmers and sugarcane workers. ▷ The norm for 1950s photographers until Castro arrived on the scene was to follow men such as Armando Hernández López, Havana's "photographer to the stars." He practiced the same type of celebrity photography that the Salases produced in New York. ▷ After his victory, Castro quickly organized Cuba's press photographers, as he did virtually every other aspect of society and politics. He understood intuitively photography's power to sway public opinion and create a desired emotional response in the viewer. For example, as a revolutionary student in 1949, Castro once bandaged his perfectly sound head in a bloodied rag to convince a photographer from the daily *Prensa Libre* newspaper that he had been injured in a street fracas with government troops. That photograph of the "injured" Fidel appeared in the next issue of *Prensa Libre* with the reactionary headline "Student Leader Assaulted by Police." ▷ Pictures of the bloody failure of Castro's 1953 and 1956 assaults on Batista's army, likewise, found their way into Cuban newspapers at crucial moments. They helped turn the tide of public opinion in favor of the ragtag guerrillas in pursuing a David-vs.-Goliath battle against the government forces. Later, while fighting in the mountains, Castro relied on the documentary skills of a small band of sympathetic international photographers, including Rene Rodriguez, Enriques Menses, Robert Taber, and Andrew St. George, a Hungarian-American who shot battle action numerous times for the stateside *Coronet* magazine. ▷ With the triumph of the Revolution, Castro the master manipulator finally realized his dream and gained full control of both the official print press and broadcast airwaves.

AT THE TIME of Castro's revolution, Havana was served by some three dozen news dailies—including two in English, two in Chinese, and one in Yiddish—and was virtually swimming in newsprint. However, eighteen months after the Revolution these publications as well as the country's five television networks were either confiscated and closed, turned into government-run operations, or squeezed out of existence through the collapse of advertising revenues. ▷ Spanish-language newspapers that disappeared included the 128-year-old *Diario de la Marina*, *Prensa Libre*, *El Mundo*, *Diario Nacional*, *El Crisol*, *El Tiempo*, *Mañana*, *Ataja*, *Pueblo*, and *Alerta*. The American expatriate community, most of them eager to leave Havana, had little time to miss the two English-language papers that perished: the sixty-year-old, conservative *Havana Post* and the progressively anti-communist *Havana Times*, the latter of which had been started in 1957 by a former FBI agent once based in Latin America. Surprisingly, there was little public outcry at the systematic dismantling of the free press in Cuba, excepting the protests of the displaced journalists. Part of the silence may be attributed to the majority of Cubans who found Castro a breath of fresh air. (A smaller percentage might have said "hot" air.) Another reason for the public's initial acceptance of a government-controlled press may be that the Cuban media had rarely been truly "free." Cuba had suffered for many decades through a procession of leaders who either forcefully suppressed or openly bribed the media into conformity and mediocrity. Batista, for instance, is said to have paid some $500,000 a month in press bribes. All but a half dozen of the country's nearly sixty newspapers were government-sponsored either directly or indirectly through thinly veiled "advertising" subsidies. One newspaper to benefit under Castro was the twenty-year-old communist *Noticias de Hoy* (Today's News). *Hoy*, the official organ of the Communist Party since 1938, had been forced to close under Batista. Now, with full funding from Castro's government, the daily paper resumed its pro-Soviet reporting with a circulation of approximately 14,000. The bigger, more influential newspaper of the first half-dozen years of the Castro regime was appropriately titled *Revolución* and was the official voice of the 26th of July Movement. *Revolución* had started in 1956 as a crude, underground mimeographed flyer under the editorship of the resourceful Carlos Franqui, shortly after Castro and Che Guevara arrived in their Sierra Maestra hideout. Had Batista's men ever found *Revolución*'s highly portable headquarters, they would

have happily dismantled the makeshift printing operation—and Franqui himself. With Castro firmly in power in Havana, *Revolución* climbed on board the first-class coach of the gravy train and grew to a six-day-a-week circulation of 100,000. Although government-funded, it at least tried to appear independent. Franqui, who was briefly an influential man with the Castro government, liked to tell visiting journalists that he and his staff had the freedom to pursue whatever stories they chose. However, even a casual observer could see that *Revolución* could never be openly

critical of Castro. Eventually, Franqui offended Fidel and became an outspoken anti-Castro exile. Once back in Cuba, Osvaldo Salas was introduced by Castro as "the Cuban photographer from New York." Franqui was impressed enough with Osvaldo's credentials to assign the just-returned exile to the directorship of *Revolución*'s photography department. At eighteen, Roberto Salas joined the ranks of the paper's top shooters, among them the famous Korda and Corrales. *Revolución* in its first year was largely visual—relying heavily on pictures by the Salases and their fellow official photographers. Roberto Salas explains the rationale for this pictorial approach, saying, "The main reason we had so many pictures in the paper was that the masses were mostly illiterate. The great majority of the people throughout the countryside couldn't read, at least until the literacy programs had time to work. And Fidel said, 'We'll tell the story of the Revolution in pictures.' We photographers saw it as a chance for big photo spreads like those in *Life* magazine. "The second reason there were so many pictures," he continues, "was that we were in a socialist state and there weren't any advertisers, so there was plenty of room to be filled." However, Cuba's "Maximum Leader" hardly invented the practice of using bold photo spreads as a tool for social reform in 1959. In highly indus-

trialized nations, where the press prides itself on "objective" journalism, there was already a seventy-five-year-old tradition of documentary photographic activism. Photographers such as Jacob Riis, Lewis W. Hine, Dorothea Lange, and W. Eugene Smith, as well as the publications that ran their work, all had hopes that pictures could sway public opinion on important social issues. The greater influence on Castro's photographic strategy for *Revolución*, however, was no doubt the documentary tradition of the Soviet Communists. From the time of Russia's October Revolution in 1917, Soviet photography was no longer created for art's sake. Pretty landscapes and painterly portraits, the kind of photography most native Cubans practiced in the 1950s, gave way to images that were powerful tools of communist propaganda. In Russia, also mostly illiterate at the time of the Revolution, massive institutions such as the People's Commissariat for Enlightenment trained countless photographers over several decades. Photography, like the other arts, became part of a great Socialist Realism scheme. According to Roberto Salas, under the less-cold-blooded Cuban socialism, strict dictates on how and what to photograph were not quite so clearly defined. Castro did not set up schools to train press photographers, nor did he issue specific photographic directions. "The government never told us what to shoot, what to do, or what not to do," Roberto Salas says flatly. "And there was no favoritism as to who got the best photo assignments. There was a group of clock-watchers at the paper, to be sure. But we six—Korda, Corrales, Mayito [Mario García Joyal, Liborio [Noval], my father, and I—worked twenty-four hours a day, seven days a week. And they gave us lots of leeway." The Revolution was well-served by a small cadre of highly motivated, already-well-trained photographic professionals (not to mention editors and writers) who believed their social movement would continue to succeed because it was in the right. The Salases and their cohorts were simply the best, most aggressive photographers in Cuba at the time. *Revolución* evolved visually into an ideological school for the masses; the photographers not only portrayed social changes but themselves inspired change. As the late photographer/historian María Eugenia Haya says of the *Revolución* newspapermen in her history of Cuban photography,

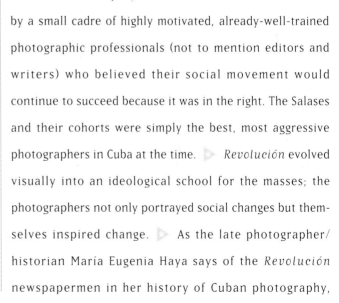

A typical front page of Revolución, *October 1959.*
(The headline reads, "Revolutionary Tribunals Will Be Reestablished Today.")

"The photojournalists traveled to the mountain ranges and united with people of the most remote areas. They were in constant movement. Photography would no more show the Cuba of the 'very nice typical mulatta' or the 'serviceable black boy,' now it would depict the bearded militia, the farmer, the worker. These new images invaded everything. Photography was used as the language to sensitize and mobilize the masses." As Castro moved his government deeper into the Marxist-Leninist camp, not every photographer and reporter remained devoted to his cause. Rogelio Caparros, a former *Hoy, Bohemia,* and *Revolución* photographer who defected in 1960 and fled to Florida with his wife, kids, dogs, and six thousand of his best negatives, was one such journalist. But as the *Revolución*-era pictures of the Salases attest, there was plenty of photographic firepower left in Cuba. Of the six main photographers for the newspaper, forty-four-year-old Osvaldo and eighteen-year-old Roberto were the oldest and youngest. Along with their peers, they documented Cuba's most dramatic modern period. The movement they started—firmly based on the importance of community and of art as a motivator for social change—still strongly influences Cuban photography to this day.

In mid-1959, *Revolución* moved from the historic Carlos III building in Havana to the larger, more modern offices of the expropriated *Prensa Libre* in the Plaza de la Revolución. Life working on the newspaper was hectic. There were several editions to put out, six days a week (excluding Sundays), all of which needed a plethora of pictures. Early daily editions were shipped to the provinces; the late edition was Havana's. Photographic supplies were then, as now, hard to come by. Film was particularly scarce, requiring creativity of the photographers before they even loaded their cameras. Nevertheless, as can be affirmed by 1950s automobiles with retrofitted diesel engines chugging through the modern-day streets of Havana, Cubans can be very resourceful. "Much of the film we shot our *Revolución* pictures with was 35mm movie film," says Roberto Salas. "What they call short-ends—the leftover spools that documentary moviemakers throw out. We'd get ten or twenty yards of the stuff at a time. We'd cut it up, load it, and would often not even know what ASA [ISO/film speed] to rate it at, or if it was Agfa, or Kodak, or what. But it did the job." For cameras and lenses, the Salases relied on 35mm workhorses they had brought from the United States: three Leicas (a highly prized M3, a 3G, and a 3F), a Nikon SP, a Nikon rangefinder camera, and the East German Hexacon that Roberto had used for his famous Statue of Liberty picture. "Our equipment was pooled. My father and I always shared our equipment. I guess in that sense you could say we were always socialists," Roberto remarks, laughing. When Eastern-bloc Communists began coming to Cuba, the photographers got a chance to pick up desirable new lenses and cameras such as Republic of East Germany Pentacons and Prakticas. Armed with these lightweight, mobile cameras, the *Revolución* shooters of the years 1959–65, called by Cubans the *fotografía épica revolucionaria,* or period of epic revolutionary photography, gave birth to modern photojournalism on their island. The vast majority of work was done in ambient light—without flash units. "We called it 'available darkness' photography," Roberto Salas says humorously.

During his career in Cuba, Osvaldo Salas's favorite setup for many of his greatest portraits was a 180mm telephoto, f/2.8 Zeiss Sonar lens screw-mounted on his Praktica camera. Osvaldo made the transition from New York studio photographer to Cuban photojournalist brilliantly. He consistently stayed on his feet longer than, and got into tight spots better than, his younger fellow *Revolución*

photographers. Because of Osvaldo's age and his permanently injured ankle and varicose veins in both legs—so advanced in later years that he had to wear special support hose day and night—this was a major achievement. By all accounts, Osvaldo toughed it out without complaint. He once matter-of-factly described to a newspaperman the prescription for his shooting style, saying "You need 5 percent technique and 95 percent imagination." Osvaldo also traveled frequently on assignment, including covering great surrealist film director Luis Buñuel on the 1959 Mexican set of *Nazarin*. He photographed Cuban ballet

sensation Alicia Alonso on countless tours. Three months after Osvaldo returned to Cuba, the Salases accompanied the Castro entourage to Washington D.C. and New York City. The Cuban leader was there to do what he has always done best: promote himself and his revolution.

SEEMINGLY EVERY AMERICAN who saw Castro on television programs such as *Meet the Press* in April 1959, and those lucky enough to come into the orbit of the Cuban leader and his band of guerrillas during their many public appearances, were charmed. It is difficult to imagine today in the wake of a decades-old embargo and cold war, but a significant number of Americans were mesmerized by the green uniform, big Havana cigar, and unruly beard. Castro was considered a romantic figure, a kind of hero. A receptive mood is captured in the remaining Salas photographs that document Castro's first official visit to the United States. But the following year, after the Salases' second trip to America accompanying Fidel, most of the thousands of negatives shot throughout 1959 by the father-and-son photography team were stolen in New York, Roberto Salas claims. It is a sobering tale of the Cold War. By August 1960, relations between Cuba and the United States were fast unraveling. Castro had already enacted his controversial agrarian-reform law and confiscated nearly 100,000 acres of formerly U.S.-owned lands in Cuba, and the United States was cancelling all imports of Cuban sugar. Most ominous of all—although it was, of course, "top secret"—the CIA began recruiting American mobsters to assist in Castro assassination plots. Roberto Salas was the only Cuban

Roberto Salas (in white shirt, far right, front row) standing atop Cuba's tallest point. Turquino Peak, with Fidel Castro and the first class of medical doctors who began their studies and graduated since the triumph of the Revolution, 1965. (Photographer unknown)

photographer allowed to photograph Castro's historic September 26, 1960, address in the United Nations General Assembly. ▷ "All hell broke loose when Fidel addressed the General Assembly," remembers Roberto. "He talked about Yankee imperialism and pissed everybody off. There was this *Life* photographer there—I don't remember who. We were sitting in the photo booth. Castro was up there talking for two hours already. The *Life* guy said, 'When's he going to stop?' And I said, 'You ain't heard nothing yet.' But the guy did let me use his 800mm lens. I put that lens on my camera, and, man, the faces were so close! I loved it. I've got a lousy habit of using other people's equipment." ▷

That month, things went sour for Roberto Salas in the United States. He thought he would be riding high as the official correspondent for *Revolución* in New York. He had set up the state-side press office for Prensa Latina, the international Latin American news agency, and even moved back to New York "to take care of business" at the small photo studio his father still owned. But after Castro's bomb-shell speech, the three large boxes of negatives that were the Salases' prized possessions were stolen from the apartment that Roberto, his mother, and his sister now shared at 60 West 76th Street. ▷ "They got 90 percent of all the stuff that my father and I shot in that first year working for Fidel," Roberto Salas says. "Among that is almost all the U.N. stuff, and an interview between Khrushchev and Fidel. Luckily, I'd left some negatives—like my Statue of Liberty shot, and the Caracas stuff with Fidel—back in Havana. I'm

guessing it was CIA, or FBI," he says. "They didn't break any windows or knock down any doors. They did a real good job." ▷ To make matters worse, the nineteen-year-old Roberto then lost his U.N. credentials. Cubans who worked for Fidel Castro were suddenly *persona non grata* in America. ▷ "I'd made some contacts among the Russians," Roberto says. "So, I got them to get me a job stringing for *Pravda* [the official Soviet newspaper]. The next Monday morning, I was a correspondent for *Pravda*, back at the U.N. with credentials. That lasted forty-eight hours. I was violating several official acts, apparently. I was an American citizen working for a foreign government. When I tried the *Pravda* number, they pulled me in, and I started feeling the pressure."

▷ Roberto Salas finally closed the New York studio he and his father had run for a decade. He sold most of his father's boxing photos to the International Boxing Commission, and the bulk of the fight negatives went to *Ring* magazine for $800. He sold the family's 4" x 5" negatives of the New York Knicks and Rangers to Madison Square Garden administrators. ▷ "Things got so bad I had to sneak back into Cuba—from New York, to Miami, to Havana," Roberto remembers. "I left a lot of stuff behind because I left in a real hurry. I showed up late one Saturday night/early Sunday morning. The Cubans were uptight at the airport about me not having papers. I tried to call *Revolución*, but there wasn't anybody there at that hour. So I told the cops at the airport, 'You can throw me in the slammer, but I'm not going back to Miami.'"

Several hours later, Carlos Franqui, the editor of *Revolución*, called and cleared Roberto. He immediately went to the hotel where his father was staying in Havana. "I walked up to the hotel—it was dawn, and the old man was out on his balcony. He said, 'What are you doing here?' I said, 'I'm back home. For good.'"   The following year, Roberto Salas obtained a Cuban passport. He would not see the United States again for thirty-eight years.

THROUGHOUT THE EARLY 1960S, the Salases covered the major Cuban events making global headlines, including Castro's sweeping agrarian-reform changes, the islandwide literacy campaign, the disastrous Bay of Pigs invasion, and the nerve-racking Russian missile crisis. (Roberto Salas's colorful remembrances fully detail those events elsewhere in this volume.)

Life in Cuba was enlivened in the 1960s by the visits of famous figures such as the novelist Gabriel García Márquez (who expressed admiration for Osvaldo Salas's work), French existential philosopher Jean-Paul Sartre, and renowned photographer Henri-Cartier Bresson. Roberto Salas chanced to meet Bresson one afternoon in the lobby of Meyer Lansky's Havana-meets-Miami mob-frequented hotel, the Riviera. He will never forget squiring Bresson on a cross-country funeral procession for Cuba's legendary singer Beny Moré, who had died that same day.   "I thought I'd really slaughtered the story of the Beny Moré funeral with my pictures for the newspaper that day. It was 1963—I was twenty-two and had a Leica and

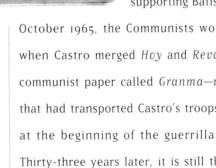

everything," says Roberto. "A couple of months later, I actually saw Bresson's photographs of the funeral in a copy of *Paris Match*. He'd gotten stuff I never even saw. So much emotion and power. And I said, 'He's the master.'"   These banner days of Cuban photojournalism soon waned. Newsprint shortages forced Castro's *Revolución* and *Hoy* to cut back drastically on the number of daily news pages, a situation most noticeable in the fewer dramatic photo spreads in *Revolución*. But it was the increasing move of Castro's government into communism, led by Marxist-Leninist Che Guevara, that spelled the real beginning of the end for *Revolución*. The paper had always identified itself as the journal of the largely apolitical 26th of July liberation movement and had long been at ideological war with *Hoy*. *Revolución* staff members even accused the communist *Hoy* of supporting Batista in the 1940s.   In October 1965, the Communists won the newspaper war when Castro merged *Hoy* and *Revolución* into one pro-communist paper called *Granma*—named after the yacht that had transported Castro's troops from Mexico to Cuba at the beginning of the guerrilla war against Batista. Thirty-three years later, it is still the official government paper.   In its heyday, *Revolución* had been photographically provocative, but it also featured surprisingly bold literary content in its widely admired but short-lived supplement, *Lunes de Revolución*, 1959–61.   Cuban newspapering became a bit more dull with *Granma*. Like many of the *Revolución* photojournalists, the Salases moved over to the new paper, with Osvaldo reprising his role as director of the photography department. But Roberto Salas went looking for a new challenge the following year—international *reportage*. ▷ To accomplish this goal, Roberto needed official credentials. He turned to his old friend Celia Sánchez, a veteran of the guerrilla warfare in the Sierra Maestra and the most powerful woman in Cuba. Roberto soon obtained permission from Fidel Castro to become the first and only Cuban correspondent to cover the Vietnam War. ▷ Over the gruelling period from 1966 to 1973, Roberto made more than a dozen trips to Vietnam, shooting for *Granma*. The newspaper often ran his pictures in big, *Revolución*-style full-page spreads. While Roberto shot some memorable portraits of Ho Chi Minh and was invited into the North Vietnamese president's home, his photographs of the ravaged landscape, of villages along the Perfume River, and of the unknown Vietnamese— mothers, children, soldiers, and other survivors—are gripping and poetic. ▷ To supplement their newspaper work throughout the '70s and '80s, both Salases shot for other publications in Cuba and elsewhere. On the island, they produced particularly strong images for the highly visual, full-color magazine *Cuba*. Roberto's work for that magazine, accompanied by the stories of well-known writers like Norberto Fuentes (now exiled), took him literally from high above the earth in Russian MiG-21 fighter jets to the bottom of Cuba's deepest copper mines. ▷ Despite his age and physical problems, Osvaldo Salas worked as hard as his son did after the days of *Revolución*, traveling with cameras to global hot spots such as Angola, Grenada,

and Panama. He also made numerous trips throughout Latin America and Europe to take photographs, participate in exhibitions, and receive awards. ▷ In later years, Cubans came to refer to Osvaldo as "*el viejo* Salas" (Old Salas), not only to distinguish him from son Roberto but to show admiration for his accomplishments. There was a major retrospective at the Museum of Fine Arts in Havana in honor of Osvaldo's seventieth birthday in 1984 and a massive traveling show in Mexico and South America in commemoration of his seventy-fifth year. The latter show featured text by the great Cuban novelist Alejo Carpentier, author of *The Lost Steps*, who wrote, "The force of human presence; the poetry of stone, and coral, the values of space, are transcended and fixed in Osvaldo Salas's masterful images." ▷ Throughout his forty-five-year career, Osvaldo Salas—who by his own estimate shot some one million pictures—received more than fifty national and international prizes. His works were seen in more than one hundred one-man and group photography shows. Yet he remained characteristically humble. ▷ "Fortunately," he told a Cuban newspaper reporter in a 1985 interview, "I think every time I am awarded a prize or am going to photograph some interesting person, I feel as nervous as when I was a youngster." ▷ Upon his death in 1992, Osvaldo Salas was sorely missed by many Cubans and friends worldwide, including the many visiting foreign photographers who had enjoyed his generosity and hospitality. ▷ Roberto Salas still gets emotional when he talks about his father. "The relation between my father and myself was much more than a father-and-son thing. I was the only boy, the eldest. And we worked the same profession. In everything he did, he consulted me. He had to call me every day on the phone, from 5 to 7 P.M." ▷ Although there was never any competition between the Salases in terms of photography, Osvaldo seemed to have expected "Bobby" to work as hard at his craft as he did. Both men employed a kind of New York "hustle" in their chosen profession—a relentless pursuit of excellence. ▷ "My father never complimented me much," Roberto admits. "He'd tell Korda or somebody else, 'Bobby did a good shot,' if he liked something I'd done. And throughout my career, I've subconsciously done things my father didn't do so I could go my own way—experimental stuff using color-slide film. He never touched that kind of thing, so that's what I did. Maybe that's why I went off to war—because he didn't care about that. In Latin American countries," he adds, "no matter what I do, I'll always be my father's son. In the old days, people would call me 'Salitas' [Little Salas, or Salas Jr.]. I always considered it diminishing. Fidel to this day calls me 'Salitas.'"

ROBERTO SALAS, a free-lance photographer since 1980, continues to shoot pictures with as much panache as ever. (He recently opened his fiftieth one-man show, featuring double-exposures of cockfights and nudes.) He works out of his home of the past twenty-five years, an airy and spacious seventh-floor apartment that he shares in Havana's Vedado section with his wife, Elvira María (whom he calls "Elvis"), his stepdaughter, and Elvira's two grandsons. The apartment is filled with awards and medals for photography that Roberto has won worldwide. In his spare time, he works in his capacity as the Caribbean region's representative for the eighty-country International Federation of Photographic Arts. ▷ As always, good equipment and supplies are nearly impossible to come by in Cuba. Roberto must either have them shipped from other countries and pay enormous taxes when they arrive (as he did recently for his new Beseler 23C III enlarger) or rely on visiting friends to bring him what he needs. ▷ Roberto says he feels sympathy for young Cuban photographers today, as there's only one place devoted specifically to photography in Havana: the Fototeca. "There are some art galleries for showing work," says Roberto, "but there aren't any schools of photography in Cuba. No place to learn it as a career. If anybody does photography, they do it out of love." ▷ Nevertheless, young Cuban photographers such as Marta María Peréz, Juan Carlos Alom, and Rene Peña have established solid reputations for themselves beyond the island. Their work, often portraying a familiar sense of community and "Cubaness," is also frequently experimental and modern, displaying abstractions and ambiguities absent in the epic '60s work of the *Revolución* photographers. ▷ Although he once traveled the world with Castro, Roberto Salas says he rarely sees the Cuban leader these days. "People ask me if I was ever close to Fidel. But that's not a photographer's place to begin with," Roberto shrugs. "As a photographer, you know you have to stay on the sidelines. Sometimes you'd spend a week with the guy. But you didn't butt in. Besides, for photographers to be successful, they have to be anonymous. You want people to forget you're there.

And with Fidel it's no exception. Today? I'm out of the press corps, and as a result, there's rarely a coincidence of us seeing each other. When I do see him, I talk to him when he talks to me. He's a busy guy." ▷ But with boxes of pictures and thousands of Castro-related negatives in Roberto's apartment, Fidel is never far away. One picture of Castro that Roberto took and says he always liked did not flatter *Jefe* himself, which gave Castro a chance to exhibit his seldom-talked-about sense of humor. ▷ "The picture is a portrait of Fidel's face. When I showed it to him and asked him to sign it, Fidel, kind of disturbed, said, 'You like this?' I said, 'Yeah.' So, now the picture's hanging in my mother's house, with Fidel's signature. He wrote on it, 'To Salitas, who likes this picture, probably because he took it.'" ▷ When asked if he feels he had been an objective news photographer for *Revolución*, Roberto shrugs again. "In photography, there are a lot of guys who say they're just observers, but I don't believe that's possible," he says. "A camera is an instrument with which you speak. To say otherwise would be like saying someone who writes a story could claim, 'I didn't say that. The typewriter did that.' You cannot say we are impartial or objective. ▷ "Nobody could say I never had anything to do with the [existing political] system," he adds. "I never belonged to the army. I was never a member of the militia. But I didn't feel they needed me there. My father and I were able to take these pictures because we loved the country and wanted to reflect the positive aspects of what we saw—not politically, but humanly. What we saw in '59, the way people lived, that wasn't good. To see these guys [Fidel, Che, and the others]

try to change things—that's what it was about. Did they find the right way? I never doubted that what they wanted was right and just as far as education and medical care goes." ▷ Roberto, speaking with his hands as he always does, spreads them wide in a sign of pragmatic resignation. "I'm not sorry I came to Cuba," he says. "My father and I worked like horses in New York and never had a nickel. I had to leave school to work. By contrast, I loved Cuba. It was new," he remembers. "I was eighteen. And three months later I was traveling the world with Fidel, taking pictures. It was easy to adapt. It was like Disneyland. And for the first time, my father was taking pictures of what he liked. Besides, we'd seen what Batista was doing. I didn't have a political name for it. Was it right? Was it wrong? I thought what I was doing was right. 'Oh, it's socialism? OK, I'm a socialist.' Now it had a name." ▷ Roberto says he does not hesitate to answer "no" when asked, as he frequently is by North American visitors, if he misses the United States. "Don't get me wrong. I'm critical of the system in Cuba," Roberto says. "But no place is perfect. Maybe if I didn't come in the way I did, at the top, I wouldn't still be here. But I choose to live in Cuba. And to other Cubans, I'm just another Cuban, from Castro on down. It's never been mentioned that I'm an American. There are things I don't agree with in Cuba. I'm not a blind bat. But you walk down the street in any city in the world—you'll find good and bad. New York? The woman who shops at Saks Fifth Avenue thinks it's great. But the guy in the slum has a different opinion. They're both right."

DOCUMENTARY PHOTOGRAPHY does not nonchalantly record life as it passes by a camera's lens. It is a form of intentional commentary on the part of the picture-maker, meant to communicate a specific message to the viewer. ▷ The documentary value of the pictures the Salases took during the life of the newspaper *Revolución* and afterward is beyond question. The photographs wholly satisfied their original purpose of informing Cuba and the world of the growth of Castro's revolutionary society. But Osvaldo and Roberto Salas were more than excellent daily-newspaper shooters. Their photographs are intimate and brimming with vitality. ▷ To study the Revolution-era photographs in this book is to be struck by how well they have stood the test of time—not merely as "documents" but as exquisite photography. Somehow the Salases captured the spirit of their subjects amidst the historically loaded settings. ▷ The noted U.S. photojournalist Lee Lockwood, himself a veteran photographer of the Cuban Revolution, said in a 1992 obituary of Osvaldo Salas for *Cuba Update.* "You can take the photographer out of the studio but you can't take the studio out of the photographer." ▷ It's a familiar axiom, but Lockwood knew it was true of the elder Salas. ▷ Roberto Salas concurs. "My father was a head-and-face man," he says. "His favorite lens was the 180 [mm telephoto]. He took portraits. But there was always something else going on behind the faces—a story." ▷ A plethora of stories dwell behind the images in this book. A prime example is Osvaldo Salas's most famous picture: the portrait of American novelist Ernest Hemingway with Fidel Castro in their only known meeting. It's a splendid example of Osvaldo Salas's unique ability to merge his well-trained studio photographer's eye with an on-the-fly news-gathering approach. How we wish we could know what the two world figures are discussing! ▷ The photographs of Osvaldo and Roberto Salas contain many subtleties and have much to say about people— legendary or forgotten, although one could argue that thanks to these images, none will be forgotten. ▷ In the final analysis, when first-rate framing and angles and the play of light and shadow are stripped away, it's their humanity that renders the Salas photographs apolitical. They are images we wish to return to, again and again. ▷ In these photographs, we see evidence of a perfect symbiotic relationship: the Salases were lucky to have dramatically charged events to photograph—not to mention dynamically photogenic subjects such as Castro, Che, Camilo Cienfuegos, and Hemingway—and Castro was fortunate too. Calling home two photographers with exceptional vision combined with skill and heart was a brilliant move on Castro's part. The brilliance of the Salases was their ability to preserve for posterity what was best in themselves.

Osvaldo Salas walking next to Fidel Castro, on assignment in Cuba, 1960.
(Photo by Omar Mendoza)

OSVALDO & ROBERTO

SALAS

ANECDOTES OF A REVOLUTION

The photo captions throughout the book
are the remembrances of Roberto Salas,
taken from interviews in Havana in 1997–98.

BEFORE THE REVOLUTION

castro in america: new york, 1955

FIDEL CASTRO'S political and revolutionary aspirations began long before his famed 1956 invasion of Cuba and subsequent two-year hiatus as a guerrilla leader in the mountains of the Sierra Maestra. ▷ The violent, politically charged atmosphere of the University of Havana, where Castro was a law student in 1945, was the real breeding ground for his career as charismatic leader and fearless defender of Cuban nationalism. ▷ During his junior year of law school, the twenty-three-year-old Castro joined an expedition to overthrow the Dominican Republic's dictator Generalísimo Rafael Trujillo. Hatched by Dominican refugees and Cuban nationals, the plot was stopped short by Cuban authorities. But Castro got the chance to cut his revolutionary teeth the following year in the rioting at the Ninth International Conference of American States in Bogotá. ▷ A vocal detractor of government corruption and U.S. domination of Cuban industries, after graduation Castro ran for Congress in the 1952 national elections. Had the election occurred and had Fidel won a congressional seat, there might never have been a Castro revolution. However, aware that he could lose his bid for the presidency, Fulgencio Batista overthrew the government three months before ballots were cast. His seemingly effortless coup was facilitated by eight years of corruption that had rotted away at the Cuban government since Batista's first reign (1933–44). ▷ Castro realized that new elections would not be called and that a dictator could only be deposed violently. The young attorney then formed an insurrection movement based on the philosophies of Cuba's great revolutionary leader José Martí. He found many sympathetic comrades. ▷ On July 26, 1953, Castro led a group of 120 rebels in an attack on Batista's army barracks in the southeastern region of Santiago de Cuba, at Moncada. It was carnival time, and Castro theorized that most government soldiers would be away on liberty—or drunk. A Batista patrol chanced upon Castro's convoy, however, and the attack ended in bloody failure. Despite being ordered to shoot Castro on sight, the lieutenant who first discovered him took Fidel to jail, saving his life. Once Castro was in confinement, Batista was forced to let him stand trial, as the revolutionary attorney had already formed a strong nationwide following. Castro served as his own defense at his trial, delivering a blistering indictment of the Batista regime. The "History Will Absolve Me" speech that served as his defense is considered a classic of modern oratory. Although Castro was sentenced to fifteen years in jail on the Isle of Pines—where his hero Martí had also been imprisoned—the rebel leader continued plotting. From behind bars, he conducted classes in political history, philosophy, and subversion, preparing for the day he would be released. That day came in early 1955, sooner than expected. In a ploy to win back waning citizen approval, Batista released all Cuban political prisoners under a congressionally approved amnesty bill. Welcomed back to Havana as a hero by many, Castro realized that things were nevertheless too dangerous for him to stay. On July 7, 1955, he left for Mexico, telling the popular opposition magazine *Bohemia,* "From such trips one does not return, or one returns with the head of tyranny at one's feet." Castro repeated his revolutionary promise in October of that year before hundreds of Cuban exiles in New York City. He was in the United States raising money for his 26th of July Movement (named after the date of the failed Moncada barracks attack) and for the first time promised publicly that he and his insurgents would attack the island of Cuba sometime in the following year. When the Argentine doctor Che Guevara met Castro in Mexico, the two men, filled with revolutionary passion, became immediate friends. Alongside such other rebel officers as Castro's brother, Raúl, they convinced themselves that their destiny was to liberate Cuba from its long history of political tyranny. On November 25, 1956, Castro delivered the promise contained in his New York speech. He led his small guerrilla band aboard a 38-foot pleasure yacht called the *Granma* and headed through the harbor waters of Tuxpan, Mexico, to his now-legendary rendezvous with Batista's army.

FIDEL IN CENTRAL PARK

NEW YORK, 1955 — Most people don't know, or have forgotten, that Fidel came to New York a couple of times (in 1949, and again in 1955) before the Revolution. My father took this picture of Fidel, clean-shaven and wearing a suit, walking in Central Park. Fidel was an attorney before he became a guerrilla. Now everybody knows him for the beard and the green uniform and hat. But in those days, raising money in New York, he looked different. He used our studio as a kind of hangout. It was on West 50th, between 8th and 9th, right across the street from the old Madison Square Garden. I used to go out and get cups of coffee for him. I was fourteen years old.

NEW YORK, 1955 — There were a lot of Cubans in New York who had come there for the same reason my grandfather had. They wanted to find better jobs since the Cuban economy was so bad. But they'd been sorry to leave Cuba, and those Cuban exiles weren't happy with Batista. Fidel was offering something better. His speech at the Palm Garden in New York was the first time he promised to invade Cuba during 1956. After his visit, the 26th of July club in New York began. People started getting serious about a revolution. The guy sitting next to Fidel at the table is the late Juan Manuel Márquez, who was the number-two man with the Revolution at the time. He later died in the 1956 assault on Batista. The Yankee dollars on the table in front of them is their take for the evening—the money they had raised for the Revolution. Today Fidel's over seventy, and he's still giving seven-hour speeches from memory. His memory is legendary. And the money photo personally

reminds me of that. During his visit to New York in '55, Fidel asked my father to make a bunch of photographic prints of the famous 1953 Moncada barracks attack. He gave us the negatives, and we made the prints at our studio. I had to deliver them to Fidel because he was leaving for Mexico the next day. When I got to where he was staying in Brooklyn, he was sitting in somebody's kitchen with this hat full of bills in front of him. Fidel said, "Thanks for the photos, kid. They're excellent." I said, "Well, my father says it's ten dollars for the box of paper we used." And Fidel said, "I'll give it to you later." I said, "Yeah, but you got money right here." And Fidel got very angry and gave me a lecture. I was just a teenager—it went in one ear and out the other. This was the first speech I ever heard him give. He was very indignant and said, "This money you see before me belongs to the Revolution. It's sacred. We can't touch that! You go tell your

father that when the Revolution triumphs, he can come back to Cuba and collect his money with glory." So, jump ahead to 1961, and I was a twenty-year-old newspaper photographer in Cuba at a meeting in the province of Montanzas, at the back of the podium with Fidel. All of a sudden this guy showed up who had been in the mountains with the Revolution. He told Fidel he'd fallen on hard times and needed a job. And Fidel promised to find him a job. But the guy was persistent. He said he needed money right away. So Fidel turned to the assembled journalists and said, "All right, everybody, dig deep and help this guy out. He was in the mountains with the Revolution." And everybody started pulling out whatever they could spare. I put my hand in my trouser pocket too, and Fidel grabbed my hand and said, "No! Not you, Salitas. I still owe you ten dollars." I couldn't believe he remembered. Of course, he still owes me the ten bucks.

NEW YORK, 1955 — Fidel Castro
in full swing at the Palm Garden.

NEW YORK, 1956 — These pictures were taken less than a year after Fidel was in New York, but already the 26th of July club was going strong. Regarding that picture of the lady with the sign, normally I don't like photos where somebody's looking right into the camera, making eye contact. Neither my father nor I took photos like that much. But sometimes it works. I think in this case, with this woman, it works. My father took pictures for the Cuban opposition press whenever he could, and he also raised money for the Movement. After Fidel's visit, my father continued to take pictures for *Bohemia*, the opposition magazine in Cuba. Under Batista, sometimes *Bohemia* was allowed to publish; sometimes it wasn't. The more Fidel did, the more serious the Cuban exiles in New York got about the Revolution.

THE STATUE OF LIBERTY

NEW YORK, August 1957 — A bunch of us young Cuban exiles were talking one day in 1957. We wanted to do something for the cause. The U.S. ambassador to Cuba had made a scene in Santiago de Cuba during a demonstration of mothers dressed in black who were protesting Batista's dictatorship. The ambassador turned his back to them and said, "What I do not see, I cannot make any comments on." Many Cubans were insulted. And we thought, "Why not put the flag of the 26th of July Movement on the Statue of Liberty? The American people will see that." At that time the Statue of Liberty was considered very sacred. So we did it. I was sixteen at the time and was nervous shooting the pictures. I put the exposed film canister in my sock. I had brought some blank rolls of film, too, ready to give to the cops, but nobody ever tried to take them. This picture made the front page of the *New York Tribune* on August 3, 1957. The *Times* ran us inside. The wire services picked it up. I sold it to UPI. *Life* magazine ran it and gave me $350. This picture has been called the most important photograph of the Revolution taken outside Cuba, because it conveyed to the people of the United States what was then our struggle for freedom. It's ironic that the picture was shot with our Hexacon, an East German camera we bought at Peerless Cameras in New York. It had a little stamp on it that said "Made in USSR Occupied Germany"—a Communist camera, if you like. At the time we'd bought it, I was ignorant of politics, so far from understanding what that little stamp meant. It's funny. I got kicked out of Carnegie Hall because of that camera too. I was taking pictures of Van Cliburn one night. He was playing the piano, and I was shooting with this 400mm lens. And everything stopped—total silence all of a sudden, a lull in the action. And that loud 35mm focal-plane shutter went off—*click!*—and echoed throughout the whole auditorium. They threw me out for the noise.

VICTORY OVER BATISTA

january 1, 1959: the real revolution begins

THE CUBAN REVOLUTION began unceremoniously on December 2, 1956, when Fidel Castro's yacht, *Granma*, ran aground in Oriente province. His cadre of eighty-one men was quickly reduced to fewer than twenty by Batista's waiting army.   As his pitiful band of rebels fanned out in disarray into the Sierra Maestra mountains of southeastern Cuba, it was a measure of the guerrilla leader's fortitude that Castro—and perhaps only he—was more convinced than ever that he would prevail over the dictator's fifty-thousand-man military.   The Cuba that Fidel, Che Guevara, and their compatriots landed in that December was one rife for revolution, and Castro knew it.   The Batista government's four years of corruption had turned the majority of Cubans into cynics sickened by an atmosphere of graft and cronyism. Batista kept a tight reign on the Congress and press. The dictator had allowed North America to maintain a stranglehold on Cuban banking and to own a large percentage of the sugar mills, tobacco companies, railroads, and utilities. U.S. mobs dominated gambling, prostitution, and pornography.   While tourists flocked to Cuba for the widely publicized sin and sun, the island's natives suffered from increasing unemployment and a recession. The middle classes were devastated by the poor economy and increasingly turned against the unconcerned president. Illiteracy ran as high as 50 percent in rural areas, and medical care, indoor plumbing, and electricity were a luxury reserved for Cuban city dwellers.   For two years, Castro confined his guerrilla warfare to the dense, difficult-to-traverse mountains of eastern Cuba, where the government army was inept at best. The rapidly spreading popularity of the exotic bearded rebels, called *barbudos*, continually eroded the dictator's power whether or not blood was being shed.   Castro continually gained recruits among destitute rural peoples, particularly since Batista's troops were unfeelingly harsh with locals when searching the mountains for revolutionaries.   The guerrillas gradually began defeating Batista's Rural Guard stations: first in La Plata, in January 1957, then Uvero, in May of the same year. In 1958, Castro's brother, Raúl, established a Second Front in northeastern Cuba. Fidel himself stepped up very effective attacks on sugar production and cut off more supply lines of commodities to urban centers. By causing shortages of basic foods and fuel, the rebels created havoc for the government.

Meanwhile, violent student actions—assassinations and bombings—prompted severe retaliation by Batista's military and police. A constant barrage of murders, atrocities, and imprisonments further turned the population against him. Conspiracies among the police, army, navy, and air force officers erupted, eating away at Batista's sovereignty. ▷ Cuba's various revolutionary fronts united behind Castro in the summer of 1958, giving the rebel army of the 26th of July Movement the green light to officially represent an anti-government offensive. Batista made one last-ditch effort to eradicate Castro and his troops in an unprecedented aerial bombardment and ground attack on the Sierra Maestras. The colossal effort failed. ▷ With Batista's regime nearing collapse, the United States ceased exporting arms to the dictator just in time to appear impartial in the revolutionary struggle. Batista, who had been embezzling enormous sums of money, tried to retain power by allowing the election of a puppet president in 1958. Even Batista's old ally Uncle Sam refused to recognize this latest figurehead. When the United States offered to install its own hand-picked successor to help put down Castro's revolt, Batista refused the gesture and sealed his

defeat. ▷ In late 1958, Castro moved out of easternmost Cuba for the first time, advancing slowly westward across the island. In stark contrast to the overpowering opposition he had faced at Moncada in 1953 and without a shot being fired, Castro found many government army barracks surrendering to his guerrillas. The rebel army increased tenfold, reaching a strength of some fifty thousand by the time Che Guevara led his celebrated liberation of Santa Clara. ▷ When Batista fled to the Dominican Republic around 2 A.M. on New Year's Day 1959, Camilo Cienfuegos and his troops advanced from Las Villas to Havana and captured Batista's command headquarters at Camp Columbia. Che Guevara secured the nearby fortress of La Cabaña. The revolt triumphed. ▷ Castro made his first victory speech at Santiago de Cuba on January 2 to loud approval. He stated, "The Revolution begins now," and started his six-hundred-mile procession across Cuba, enjoying rapturous ovations the entire way. ▷ Although Castro immediately named Manuel Urrutia the provisional president of Cuba, he forced the political straw man out of office five months later. Few Cubans doubted who really ran the country; *Jefe*'s name was Fidel Castro.

THE TRIUMPH OF THE REVOLUTION

HAVANA, 1959/1961 — This picture was taken on the day of the first official 26th of July celebration, the only one Camilo Cienfuegos got to see. He wanted to stop for a coffee and look at the *Revolución* newspaper in a little café. Camilo had been a simple man, a tailor, but became an important guerrilla leader in the Revolution. He was the head of the vanguard, a real hero. Later that year, he was lost in a plane somewhere at sea. He died for the same reason he was a great revolutionary fighter—he was fearless. The day he died, the pilot did not want to take off from Camagüey because of foul weather. Camilo insisted he had to be flown back to Havana. And who's

going to tell Camilo no? We think they flew out to sea to avoid the storm over the island. Fidel and Che joined the aerial search for them for three days, but they never found anything. At right, the spirit of the Revolution lives on in the slogan *Patria o Muerte* ("Patriotism or Death"), seen in this sign in the crowd. Victory signs were everywhere in Cuba after Castro finally won. The day after the Revolution was a success, I was on a plane—January 2, 1959—at New York's Idlewild Airport with my camera bag and a bunch of other crazy Cuban Americans. Everybody's going home! It was an adventure—guns, bombs. I didn't know politics. You

have no idea of the euphoria of that moment. There were guys on the plane with big guns, boxes of hand grenades, bazookas on the seats. At Idlewild! It was all stuff they'd been saving for the 26th of July Movement, for a possible invasion of the island. I have no idea what they thought they were going to do with all that stuff when they got to Cuba. The Revolution had already succeeded. When I got down there, I ran into Fidel on his first day back in Havana—January 8, 1959. We were at a television studio, and he said, "Salitas, how's your old man? How's his legs? Tell him to come down." My father showed up in Havana with his camera a week later.

HAVANA, January 1959 — This photo was taken the week after the Revolution was successful. Fidel had come into Havana victorious on January 8 after a Roman-style march across Cuba. He'd taken over the old Presidential Palace, and there were soldiers everywhere, sleeping in all the rooms. That week I was living in the darkroom at the Palace, which had been there since Batista's time. I could have stayed upstairs in one of the rooms with the guerrillas, but I slept on a table in the darkroom, because I had the place to myself, it was cooler down there, and there were no mosquitoes. I used my spare clothes as a pillow. It was probably January 10. I woke up at three or four o'clock in the morning. I couldn't sleep, so I went upstairs to see if anything was happening. I walked into this big room, and there's Fidel and Che in an intense conversation, fixing the world. Those guys would talk strategy all night. There were no lights on. But Fidel was getting out a fresh cigar. I had one of our old Leicas in my hand, and I just walked up, braced it against the table in front of them, and made a one-second exposure while he was lighting up. It means a lot to me because it's the first picture I ever took of Che, the first time I met him. The week after that I was off on my first trip out of the country with Fidel, taking pictures in Venezuela.

HAVANA, 1959 — This *guerrillero* is riding his bicycle through the Presidential Palace on the marble floors, something he never could have done when Batista was in power.

GUERRILLAS ON HORSEBACK

HAVANA, 1959 — For the first 26th of July celebration after the triumph of the Revolution, Fidel wanted to re-create the guerrillas' New Year's Day journey into Havana. So, several months later Camilo rode back into town on horseback leading the *campesinos* (peasants) from the countryside. They came by the hundreds, on horseback, on flatbed trucks, carrying the Cuban flag. The picture below has a black border. It's one I've printed lately. The one at right is a vintage print made when I was back in New York in the '60s, before I started printing with borders. The reason I started using the borders in the first place, in the '80s, is I'd print pictures for people in Latin American countries, and maybe they don't have money for a frame. This way, they can just hang it on the wall.

LEADING MEN AND WOMEN OF THE REVOLUTION

HAVANA, 1959 — Here are Fidel and Che with Raúl Castro (center) in a spur-of-the-moment meeting. They were the biggest names of the Revolution. Raúl is Fidel's brother, but he earned his way in the Revolution. He was in the Moncada barracks attack, in prison with Fidel on the Isle of Pines, and on board the *Granma* for the 1956 invasion of the island. He fought alongside Fidel and Che and Camilo throughout the Revolution. Women fought too. Celia Sánchez is seen in the photo at left, resting on a jeep and talking to the head of a female security force (wearing beret and sidearm). The female combat group during the war against Batista was called the Mariana Grajales Platoon (named after a black woman combatant in Cuba's first war of independence). They took some casualties in the fighting. Celia was with the Revolution from the time she met Fidel in 1957. There's no ques- tion that she was the most powerful woman in Cuba. After the triumph of the Revolution, Celia was Fidel's secretary and took care of big things and little things. I remember when Fidel was in Chile on official business, Celia talked to him every day on the phone for two, two and a half hours. One evening he was hoarse. She told him to be sure to take some aspirin and gargle with salt water. But she would just as likely discuss matters of state.

HAVANA, 1959 — This group of people have taken over a train and are celebrating Castro's victory. The Shell Oil sign beside the train, like the American company that owned it, would soon be removed from Cuban soil.

HAVANA, 1970 — The spirit of the Revolution
is still reflected in the face of this woman,
years after Fidel's victory, as she holds a
Granma newspaper above her head.

THE MONUMENTAL PHOTO

CARACAS, January 1959 — This picture was taken three weeks after the Revolution was victorious. Fidel was on tour in Venezuela. Some people have said they like this photo because it's shot looking up at Fidel, who looks "monumental" with the flag and everything, as if he's already a statue. But that was accidental—literally. I arrived at the airport in Caracas and it was jam-packed with people. Somebody on Fidel's truck shouted for me to get on board because he was taking off. But this Venezuelan soldier who didn't know me from Adam hit me in the stomach with his rifle butt. There were some tense moments and then they sorted it out and this guy realized I was OK after all. So the Cuban soldiers pulled me up onto the bed of the truck and it took off. I couldn't even sit up, I was in so much pain. But I thought, "Well, everybody at the newspaper back home's going to want to know where my pictures are." So I lay on my back and started shooting. That's why the angle. It wasn't intentional. I was lucky to get this at all.

PLAZA OF THE REVOLUTION

HAVANA, 1963 — Fidel is speaking to a convention of sugarcane cutters. You can see a mural on the wall of the building over his shoulder showing the cane fields. It says that the goal is "...to turn into sugar all the cane fields of Cuba."

HAVANA, 1959 — Farm workers at a public meeting raise
their machetes in solidarity amid a show of Cuban flags.

FIDEL AND THE PEOPLE

1959 — At left, Fidel has on his back one of the Belgian rifles that the chief of the Venezuelan army sent to him when he was fighting in the Sierra Maestras. Fidel really liked that rifle a lot. He ordered a bunch more. Even though the United States didn't want foreign countries selling arms to Cuba, the Belgians sent a whole shipload of weapons in early 1960. The ship, *Le Coubre*, was in Havana harbor for only a week when it mysteriously blew up, destroying Fidel's rifles with it. Eighty-two people were killed. Nobody could pin the explosion on anybody for sure, but we think it was the work of the CIA. The picture above was taken in a peasant shack in the Sierra Maestras by available light. It's a vintage photo I printed back in the 1960s. I printed all our photos. My father did not like to print. When we were living in New York, he got sick of working in the darkroom. When you have to print a hundred sports publicity photos of the same shot at a time, you get sick of printing. Anyway, I don't know where the negative to this shot of the peasants is. It's been lost.

1959 — This overhead shot shows the Capitol building in Old Havana. The building is based on the U.S. Capitol. The shot at right shows the 26th of July parade along the famous oceanfront boulevard of the Malecón, with El Castillo del Morro in the background.

HAVANA, 1966 — May Day celebration.

CASTRO'S U.N. HONEYMOON

NEW YORK, April 1959 — This is a rare happy moment at the United Nations for Fidel. Actually, it was happy because the U.N. wasn't in session. We were there in the spring, and the Assembly is something like September to January. It was his first trip back to the States, only two months after the Revolution. I found myself back in America too, still a teenager. The first one off the plane when we landed in Washington D.C. was me, then Fidel. This was the year he didn't speak at the U.N. He was just there visiting. Everybody in New York loved him. He sat at the table where the CUBA sign is. Of course, the next year when Fidel visited the U.N. officially, he wasn't such an easy bone to chew. I covered that too. I was the only Cuban photographer with credentials allowed in the General Assembly. That was the year Fidel blasted U.S. imperialism and monopolies for four hours. The year Khrushchev started banging his shoe on the podium. The rest, as they say...

LAND REFORM

LA PLATA, 1959 — This was taken at Fidel's former mountain hideout in the Sierra Maestras on May 17, 1959. It was a historic moment because he had chosen his old headquarters to finish up the Agrarian Reform Law (the papers lying on his chest), which was the first big change in Cuba after the triumph of the Revolution. Under the agrarian reform, Fidel broke up the *latifundios* (big estates), greatly restricting the size of land anyone could own. The opposition didn't think he'd have the nerve to do it. Eventually, in August 1960, foreign properties in Cuba were seized. That pissed off the American companies and the U.S. government. After that, a lot of upper- and middle-class property-owning Cubans left for Miami.

WASHINGTON D.C., 1959 — In Washington D.C., the *guerrilleros* really enjoyed themselves visiting the Washington Monument and the Lincoln Memorial (shown here). The guy on the left is Camilo Cienfuegos. Everybody in America had a crewcut then, but not these guys. The long hair and beards were a badge of courage. In Cuba, we called them the *barbudos* (bearded ones). If you had that look, it meant you'd been in the mountains with Fidel. Of course, they wore their hair and beards that way because they had been in the mountains for a long time. Up there, shaving is a pain in the ass. And the hair is convenient against the sun, bugs, and mosquitoes. That was the first time that long hair and beards became a symbol of protest. The American college kids and hippies in the '60s picked up on it from the Cubans.

SAN LORENZO, 1960 / CAMAGÜEY, 1961 — This girl (left) is one of the young people who volunteered as a teacher in the great literacy program that went from the cities out into the provinces to educate the masses. There were thousands of student-teachers like her. And they'd teach kids to teach other kids. She's standing in a thatched hut that served as the "school" for the farmers around San Lorenzo. The members of the brigade went out into the farthest rural areas and, after winning the confidence of the people, taught them to read. The blonde girl with the flag (below) is an education-brigade member in Camagüey. Until students like her taught people to read, Fidel used *Revolución*, with its picture spreads, to tell the story of the Revolution visually. He also went on television two or three times a week to explain different situations.

FIDEL UP ON THE MOUNTAIN

PICO TURQUINO, 1965 — These two pictures commemorate the first class of doctors who began their studies and graduated since the Revolution succeeded. Before Fidel took over, medical care was not free in Cuba. Poor people could not get treated. So it was a big deal to have all these new doctors graduating. They asked Fidel to be the guest of honor for the graduation. And typical of Fidel, he said he would do it—but the graduation ceremony would have to be at the top of Pico Turquino (7,300 feet), the highest mountain peak in Cuba. Now, this is not like going to the Copacabana. You had to climb to the top of that mountain. Some of Fidel's troops from the Revolution were going to take the hike. And Che's wife made that trip too. (That's Celia Sánchez in the middle of the pack, without a hat.) Unfortunately for me, I was already in the mountains. I'd spent three weeks shooting pictures for the newspaper in the Sierra Maestras without changing my socks. I had really painful foot problems. And then Fidel wanted me to shoot these pictures of the doctors graduating on top of the Turquino. In desperation, I had a doctor bandage my feet. As the photographer, I had to stay ahead of Fidel all the way up to take photos. One thing about Fidel, he's a slow walker, but that guy never stops. He doesn't stop to drink water. He doesn't stop to go to the bathroom. He covers a lot of ground. And I had to stay ahead of him the whole way. It was a five-and-a-half-day hike. I never want to do that again as long as I live. The picture of the pretty woman with the rifle? She's one of the doctors who graduated. About 25 to 30 percent of the graduating class was female. That bust of José Martí she's standing beneath was carried up to the top of the mountain in 1952, before Fidel's first attack on Batista, by Celia Sánchez and her father, who was also a doctor.

CELIA SÁNCHEZ

HAVANA, 1968 — This picture was taken in the office of the director of the newspaper *Granma*, where there was a big painting of Che based on one of my father's photos. Celia never liked having her picture taken, so we had to get informal portraits of her. Che was killed in Bolivia the year before this photo was taken. I was in Vietnam at the time, working as the Cuban correspondent for *Granma*. It was something I really wanted to do, and Celia, as Fidel's confidante, got me the clearance to go and be a war correspondent. When I went to Vietnam, Celia gave me a black Rolex Submariner watch inscribed on the back "To Salas." I've still got it. She was a great woman. Ever since Celia died of cancer in 1980, nobody's been able to take her place.

CASTRO, THE MAN

*on pitcher's mound, with papa hemingway,
in the pulpit, with the people*

AGAINST ALL ODDS, Fidel Castro has remained the "Maximum Leader" of Cuba for forty stormy years. A brilliant and charismatic man, and a master of oratory and manipulation, Castro has kept his tiny tropical island at the forefront of headlines and history. In doing so, he has become the most consistently interesting modern world leader—which is not to say he is the most universally admired. ▷ There have been dozens of attempts on Castro's life—a fair number of them overseen by the CIA. While many of those assassination plots involved guns and bombs, the most outrageous scheme called for a key Castro aide to dust the leader's combat boots with a powder that would cause his beard to fall out, thereby discrediting Fidel with his people. Despite these efforts, Castro, like the spirit of the Cuban people, endures. ▷ Born August 13, 1926, at a well-appointed *finca* (plantation) in the legendary far-eastern Oriente province, Fidel Alejandro Castro Ruz was exceptional from childhood. His father, a physically powerful and determined former Spanish soldier, rose from near poverty to own some 25,000 acres and most of the buildings in the small town of Birán, Cuba. He was not overtly political, yet Castro's father was powerful enough to control most of the local sugarcane, in addition to dealing in cattle and timber. He instilled in his seven children a deep respect for the poor and for the Cuban land. ▷ Large and strong, Castro in his elementary-school days earned a reputation as a fighter who refused to back down from the cruelest bullies. He excelled in all sports (particularly baseball and basketball) and was voted the best all-around Cuban athlete in 1943–44. Castro exhibited such prodigious mental skills that his classmates in the nation's best Jesuit schools swear to this day that he memorized entire textbooks with seemingly no effort. ▷ While attending law school at

Havana University, Castro rose quickly to the upper ranks of the violent campus politics characteristic of that period. Long before graduation, though, he had set his sights on a much larger goal: the leadership of Cuba itself. Castro's personal obsession was no less than to become the successor to his great idol, José Martí, the national hero of Cuba, who died fighting for independence from the Spanish in the 1890s. Even in law school, Castro earned a national reputation as one of the men most likely to succeed in deposing Cuba's corrupt president, Fulgencio Batista. ▷ After the success of his revolution, a victorious Castro visited the United States on April 17, 1959, meeting with American Vice President Richard Nixon. In answer to Nixon's suspicions, Castro denied that his government was communist. ▷ A year later, however, Castro moved against what he called "U.S. economic aggression." Castro nationalized American-owned oil refineries, sugar mills, utility plants, and other properties worth hundreds of millions of dollars, precipitating a U.S. economic embargo that is in force to this day. ▷ Since that time, Castro has survived the famed Bay of Pigs invasion, the Cuban Missile Crisis, a disastrous war in Angola, the exodus of some 120,000 Cubans in the Mariel "boatlift" to Miami, and even the fall of the Soviet Union. Today, deprived of support from the Soviets worth billions of dollars annually that formerly propped up the Cuban economy, Castro is leading his nation of eleven million through what he calls "the Special Period." ▷ Throughout it all, though the people are poor and everything including food is rationed, the majority of Cubans still appear to support Castro. ▷ Whether he is giving memorized hours-long speeches on the importance of remaining communist or hosting the pope, as he did in early 1998, Fidel Castro is still very much Cuba's Maximum Leader.

FIDEL SMOKES

1961 — This one is immediately recognizable. Although you see just Fidel's nose and beard, you know it's him. My father, being a head-and-face man, liked to come in extra-close sometimes with the telephoto. They made a poster out of this in France years ago. It was called "Viva Castro."

WITH PAPA HEMINGWAY AND THE PEOPLE

BARLOVENTO, 1960/SIERRA MAESTRAS, 1959— The shot to the left is, of course, from the one time that Fidel and Hemingway officially met, in 1960, a year before the famous writer killed himself back in the United States. It's no secret that Hemingway's writing really impressed Fidel. There's a well-known story that Fidel once said he learned guerrilla warfare from *For Whom the Bell Tolls*. Hemingway had been living on the island on and off for twenty years when this was taken, so it's odd he and Fidel had never met before that. My father took this shot on the occasion of the Tenth Annual Hemingway Fishing Tournament, at the Barlovento Yacht Club. Originally, Fidel was only supposed to hand out the winning trophy. But, sportsman that he is, he entered the tournament and caught the biggest marlin of the day, so Hemingway ended up giving *Jefe* the trophy. I say it's from their one "official" meeting, because I heard that Fidel had once said that he'd met Hemingway a second time. He said that he'd been invited out to the writer's home, *finca Vigía*, and that he accepted and spent hours out there, late into the night. I wish I could tell you what they talked about, but now only Fidel knows. In the picture of Fidel with the people (above), he's visiting the mountains where he fought in the Revolution. You'll notice he has two wrist watches on. That's the way he wore them in the mountains. He's such a precise guy. He wore two watches so if one stopped he'd still be able to be synchronized with the other rebels.

1959 — Fidel back in the Sierra Maestras.

APRIL 1959 — This picture pretty much sums up Fidel's first visit to the States after he won the Revolution. He's standing on a hotel balcony across the street from Grand Central Station. That's the American flag behind him. He's waving to a crowd of Americans, and they acted glad to see him. They were fascinated by him anyway, even if they didn't know quite what to make of him.

SANTIAGO DE CUBA, 1962 — This is from one of the annual 26th of July celebrations, the ninth one since the Moncada army barracks attack against Batista. Fidel (with Cuban President Dorticos to his right) is standing over a portrait of the late Russian Communist leader Lenin. Fidel's speech that day was a little over a year after the Bay of Pigs invasion, and he predicted that the United States would invade Cuba again. He also said that he'd acquired new weapons to protect Cuba from Uncle Sam. We didn't know at the time that the Missile Crisis would soon be upon us.

Vintage photos, printed in the 1960s.

UNDER THE CLOUDS

SANTIAGO DE CUBA, July 1964 — The ability
of Fidel to mesmerize a crowd from the
speaker's platform is legendary. There are
many stories about his powers of oratory.
The first night I ever saw Fidel on Cuban
soil, January 8, 1959, he gave his first victory
speech in Havana. The speech lasted nearly
all night, but the streets remained jammed
with thousands of people. At one point, a
dove—a magical symbol in Santeria—landed
on Fidel's shoulder and just sat there peace-
fully for a long time. The crowd was stunned.
But even without doves, he's a magnetic
speaker. What strikes me about this picture
is the drama of the sky behind him, which
seems to match the intensity of his speech.

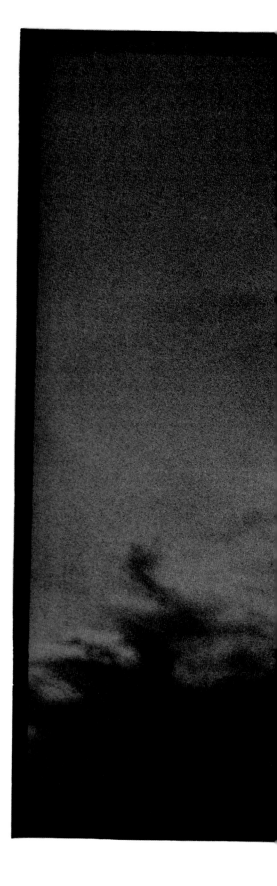

1961 — Fidel thinking, then directing the troops.

MEETING WITH STUDENTS AND FARM FAMILIES

1965 — It might seem hard to believe to some people today, but in the '50s and '60s, the Cuban people had incredible access to Fidel, Che, Camilo, and Raúl. They went everywhere. And anyone could walk up to them and talk to them. Plus, Fidel went to the mountains often to take the pulse of the people. Those farmers in the Sierra Maestras have always been able to talk to Fidel like nobody else could, because Fidel knows them by name. I've seen guys talk to Castro and tell him off. I saw a guy waving at Castro once during one of our trips to the Sierras. The guy kept trying to get Fidel's attention. Fidel stopped his speech and said, "Why don't you let me talk?" The guy said, "It's important!" Fidel said, "But you're being disrespectful." And the guy said, "I've been listening to you the last couple of years waiting for you to stop talking. Now it's my turn." Fidel put his arm around him and they walked off under a tree. Fidel sits down and the guy is standing over him. He's really getting stuff off his chest. This was one of the guys who fed Fidel and hid him out in the old days. But then, the Sierras are Fidel's favorite place, where the Revolution started. Those rural places were the first he gave schools and roads, to pay those people back. Plus, they were in the worst condition to begin with. They didn't have any electricity, water, medical. Nothing.

1970 — Fidel first came up with the idea that everybody should put in some time cutting sugarcane in 1965. He wanted Cuba to be number one in sugar production. He took it seriously. And when he said everybody should cut cane, he meant *everybody*. He took the whole Council of Ministers out to Camagüey to cut cane for a week. And as this picture shows, he got in there himself. Actually, I think Fidel's pretty disconnected from material things in general. He always lived pretty simply when I knew him. I've got another story about that, too. My first wife's father owned a café next to one of the famous radio stations where Fidel hung out in the old days. With Fidel it was always "Give me a *café con leche* and toast. Put it on my bill." After the Revolution, my father-in-law gave me Fidel's bills he'd signed for. This guy never had a dime. And he didn't care.

ANOTHER CIGAR

1965 — Here's Fidel with his favorite prop
again: the cigar. Actually, he stopped smoking
in the '80s sometime. It was supposed to be a
good health example for the people. At least
he quit smoking. I'm not sure anybody else did.

RELAXING IN THE SIERRA MAESTRAS

1965 — These are two of my favorite shots I've taken of Fidel at rest. They were both taken on the trip up the mountain for the graduating class of doctors. The day I took the hammock picture, Fidel roasted a piece of meat on a long stick and then started offering it around. He gave some to Celia Sánchez. He offered me some. He gave it all away and never had any himself. While taking the shot below, Fidel told me, "Salitas, don't take my picture with my shirt off." I took it anyway. And I like it. Hell, it was hot up there. It's good to take your shirt off if you can. The dog in front of Fidel was his German shepherd, Guardián. He loved that mutt; he went everywhere with him in those days—even to the top of Cuba's highest mountain.

HAVANA, 1966 — Everybody knows that Cubans love baseball. And Fidel's no exception. He'd just show up at Cerro, the big baseball stadium in Havana, and pitch an inning. In this shot of him pitching under the lights, he's still got on his green army fatigue pants and combat boots. The rebels had a team called the *Barbudos* (bearded ones), with their own jerseys and everything. In the picture of Fidel batting, that's an old American Louisville Slugger in his hands. Some people have said recently that Fidel tried out once and didn't make one of the U.S. pro teams, the Washington Senators. I never heard that before. I can't confirm it or deny it.

1966/1970 — The photo below shows you
Fidel up-close and personal, speaking at the
26th of July event in 1966. The one on the
right is a bird's-eye view I took over the Plaza
de la Revolución in 1970. That's Fidel right
down there up front—the center of attention.

CHE GUEVARA

the revolutionary as cult figure

EVERYWHERE ONE LOOKS in modern-day Cuba, there are tributes to the island's secular patron saint: the revolutionary hero Che Guevara. ▷ Che's fiercely proud eyes gaze out from posters enshrined in the vestibules of private homes along the streets of Old Havana. His stoic face beneath a star-clad beret—instantly recognizable throughout the world—is silk-screened on T-shirts sold in public squares and stenciled in rainbow colors on whitewashed walls. His portrait, five stories high, dominates a government building in the Plaza de la Revolución. ▷ All of these images, as well as the slogan chanted by Cuban university students and true-believers, "Seremos Como Che" ("We will be like Che"), testify to the incredible staying power of the long-martyred revolutionary. ▷ Although Fidel Castro has been the undisputed leader of Cuba since 1959, it's doubtful that his government or the country itself would have become what it has but for his fateful meeting with the young Argentine doctor in Mexico in late 1955. Castro was twenty-nine, Guevara twenty-seven. Before that historic occasion, both men had been preparing for revolution in their differing but equally determined ways. ▷ Born of Spanish-Irish descent to a once-prominent central Argentine family on June 14, 1928, Ernesto Guevara de la Serna was afflicted with severe asthma at the age of two. The boy's relentless dedication to overcoming his disease—by becoming both a scholar and an athlete—forged the iron will that would make him a legendary combatant in guerrilla warfare. ▷ Even before receiving his medical degree in 1953, Guevara was a frequent and observant traveler throughout Latin America, where he was moved by the widespread poverty. This experience confirmed in Guevara the unshakable belief that Latin America could only find freedom and fulfill its true destiny through armed struggle against capitalist imperialism. ▷ Guevara first attempted to practice his revolutionary principles in Guatemala. His loathing of U.S. policies was only strengthened by the 1954 CIA-supported coup overthrowing the Arbenz regime's socialist revolution in that country. The young Guevara moved on to Mexico City, where he met and befriended Fidel Castro and his brother, Raúl, then assembling a guerrilla force to attack the army of Cuban dictator Batista. ▷ In November 1956, Guevara sailed with the Castros and seventy-nine other men to Cuba. Although wounded early in the fighting there and frequently plagued by asthma attacks, Guevara proved a courageous warrior more than equal to the revolutionary dogma that had dominated his conversation for years. ▷ As Castro gained momentum and converts in the mountains of the Sierra Maestra, Guevara rose to the guerrillas' top ranks, alongside the Cuban-born Castro brothers and Camilo Cienfuegos. His Cuban comrades called Guevara by his now-infamous nickname, alluding to his constant punctuation of sentences with the characteristically Argentine interjection *che* ("hey, man"). ▷ On January 2, 1959, the day after Batista fled Cuba, Guevara entered Havana with Cienfuegos and hundreds of troops. The Argentine hero proudly assumed control of the city's fortress La Cabaña. ▷ Named "supreme prosecutor" in the trials of those accused of war crimes during the revolutionary struggle, the guerrilla hero displayed cool detachment in overseeing the execution of dozens of former *Batistianos.* ▷ Soon perceived as second only to Castro himself, Guevara was handed plum assignments such as heading the industrial department of the National Institute for Agrarian Reform and serving as president of the National Bank of Cuba. In the latter role, Guevara's intense focus on industrialization over agriculture spelled economic disaster for Cuba for many years to follow. More successful were his voluntary work programs, which encouraged every Cuban to selflessly devote time to public works, as Guevara himself did every weekend. ▷ Guevara also helped push Fidel Castro further into a Marxist-Leninist form of government, a move that eventually undermined Che's influence. As Castro's government became increasingly controlled by Soviet Communists, who Guevara, now a Cuban citizen, considered undisciplined and bureaucratic, he became anxious. He longed for the direct conflict with imperialism that only far-flung guerrilla warfare could provide. ▷ Dropping out of public life in 1965, Guevara eventually traveled to Africa to spend time aiding the unsuccessful revolutionary struggle there. ▷ Guevara made a brief, secret reappearance in Cuba to meet with Castro the following year. Shortly thereafter, convincingly disguised with close-shorn gray hair, glasses, and the attire of an elderly businessman, Guevara moved to Bolivia in a final attempt to export his revolutionary tactics. After eleven months of frustration, during which he won neither Bolivian communist support nor that of the rural "oppressed," Guevara found himself and his small band of men hounded by government soldiers and the CIA. ▷ On October 8, 1967, Guevara and his guerrillas were finally hunted down and captured in the rugged south-central part of the country. The next day, Cuba's expatriate hero was executed by a government agent on the dirt floor of the dilapidated Bolivian schoolhouse where he had been held prisoner. Guevara's martyrdom, already guaranteed, was intensified by the fact that he was just thirty-nine years old. In college dorm rooms worldwide, Che became the poster boy for all forms of opposition to "the establishment." In seemingly every country, he was a mythologic figure and a source of inspiration and determination to oppressed peoples. ▷ Though Guevara's body was thrown into an unmarked grave, bones believed to be his were finally found and returned to Cuba with much ceremony in 1997. His final resting place is now in his adopted country, in the central Cuban city of Santa Clara, site of his greatest anti-Batista battle victory. ▷ The romanticism that surrounds the legend of Che Guevara today manifests itself in laudatory books, Hollywood movies, and the angst-ridden lyrics of rock-and-roll songs of several continents. Radicals from Northern Ireland to the Sahara idolize Guevara as a model for modern revolution. ▷ By all accounts, even among Cuban exiles who disdain the Castro regime, few have ever lived up to Guevara's example. He is a man who never compromised his principles.

BLOWING SMOKE

SANTIAGO DE CUBA, July 26, 1964 — My father used his 180mm lens for this portrait, which is his most famous picture of Che. It was a lucky shot, as my father used to say. He moved around behind the table where Che was sitting at the speech for the 26th of July, and the lights that had been set up for the television cameras were shining through his cigar smoke, backlighting him. It was a rare moment.

HAVANA, 1960 — This is Che with his daughter, Hildita, his first child, when she was four years old. You can see her resemblance to her father. She died in 1995 at the age of thirty-nine, the same age as Che. The other soldier holding her hand is Antonio Nuñez Jiménez, who worked closely with Fidel.

| 1960 — Che and Fidel at the airport in Havana.

AT THE TELEVISION STUDIO

HAVANA, 1960 — This is Che in a typical moment, looking concerned. He was the most intense guy I ever met, always a kind of outsider. People forget that he was Argentine, and they generally aren't as open as Cubans. Che always felt he had a hard time fitting in. And he was always obsessed by thinking about the revolutionary struggle. Che was great at analyzing global and political situations. But he wasn't a good judge of character, and I think he knew it. He believed in a way of life, and a society, the State, that was too far ahead of his time. He came up with this idea that society should do away with money, that we should use a barter system. It's a beautiful idea, but it would never work. Still, he didn't accept any variation from his goals. He was capable of doing anything necessary to convince people he was right. When Che finally left the country, the CIA tried very hard to make it look like there was a split between Che and Fidel—that Che was pro-Chinese and Fidel was pro-Russian, that Che was Argentine and Castro was Cuban. But the facts are completely the other way around. Castro trusted Che more than just about anybody.

CHE AT SEA

STRAITS OF FLORIDA, 1960 — My father shot these pictures of Che during the Hemingway marlin-fishing tournament. When my father got back from the trip, he had not taken many photos—which was not characteristic of him. I asked the photographer Korda, "How come the old man didn't take too many pictures?" Korda said, "Poor guy, he got seasick pretty soon after we went out and was down below for most of the trip." Yet I like these photos of Che reading. He loved books of all kinds. What do you suppose he's reading? Marx? Or maybe it's Hemingway. In the shot below, that's Fidel leaning over him. Fidel was more interested in fishing than Che was.

HAVANA, 1961 — Che came up with the idea of Cuba having voluntary work days to rebuild the country. People were supposed to give half a day on Sunday to do public works. And he worked harder than anybody—he really got down in the mud. Che didn't care about being number one or number two. He was there to do what Castro—as the leader of the country—couldn't do. On one of the first of these work days, Liborio Noval, one of the *Revolución* photographers, showed up to say hello. He was dressed in his Sunday clothes.

And Che said, "You ready to work?" Liborio said, "No, I can't. I'd mess up my clothes." And Che said, "Yeah, but you should work anyway." And so, he got Liborio in there in the dirt with him, worked him for hours, and completely ruined his suit. The next Sunday morning, Che went over to Liborio's and asked him if he was going to wear his suit again for the volunteer work day. The picture on the right I call "Muddy Boots." It was taken by my father on one of those voluntary work days when they were doing a

construction project. The negative I printed this from hasn't survived well, like a lot of them. The negative is so thin you can see through it. Some of my father's negatives, like the ones he shot of Batista in New York in 1952, were eaten by termites. But I still get good prints out of this one, even if I have to touch it up by hand. Raúl Corrales, one of my fellow *Revolución* shooters, looked at some of my old negatives one day and said, "From this you can pull prints?" Corrales said I was the greatest printer in Cuba.

IN THE PUBLIC EYE

HAVANA, 1962/1963 — The picture on the left is Che speaking before the CTC (Central Organization of Cuban Trade Unions). Guevara was the hero of the common man in more ways than one. In the picture above, that's a cheapo cigar he's smoking. Che smoked the cheapest cigars possible, the ones we call *cazadores*. They cost something like ten cents apiece. Of course, he could have smoked any brand he wanted. But he didn't want to waste the money. He smoked a lot, and he had some idea that tobacco smoke was good for his asthma. But then, everything Che did he did his own way, for his own reasons.

THE CHRISTLIKE CHE

HAVANA, 1963 — This is one of our most
powerful pictures of Che. Here, he's almost
Christlike, which is a comparison some
people have made.

HAVANA, 1964 — Few people remember that Che made some money early in his career taking pictures. He loved to look at any new cameras we might have, and they say he had four rolls of undeveloped film in his pack when they finally caught up with him in Bolivia. But in front of the camera, he was really a pretty private guy. He kept his distance and was shy about publicity. Once in '63, I arrived late at a reception out in the garden of one of the foreign embassies, where Che was dining. They'd just turned off the hot lights for the television cameras, and of course I didn't have a flash. I never had a flash in those days. It was "available darkness" photography. So I told the *luminito* (lighting man), "Turn 'em back on—I gotta get some pictures." The guy turned the lights on, and I went right up to Che and started shooting with the Nikon. He glared at me, stopped eating, got up, and took my camera. "Sit down and start eating," he said. Well, you don't argue with Guevara. So I sat down and started eating. And Che shot my entire roll of film—of me eating. He finished the roll and said, "You got any more film?" I said, "No, I just got the one roll." I was really embarrassed by this point, because there was an ambassador there. Che handed back my camera and said, "Good. Now you can get out of my chair, Salas. Having your picture taken's a pain in the ass, ain't it?"

1963 — Che waving to the crowd
at the May Day celebration.

1964 — Che making a point with his cigar,
which he often did.

MEMORIAL MURAL FOR CHE

HAVANA, October 17, 1967 — Che was hunted down and killed in Bolivia on October 9, 1967. We didn't know it at the time in Cuba. A week later, the rumor of his death started circulating around Havana. I went to the newspaper and verified it. Fidel went on television twenty-four hours later and told everyone. They didn't want to believe it at first. Everybody had been waiting to hear it from Fidel. The night of the speech to commemorate Che's death, more than one million people paid tribute to him in the Plaza de la Revolución. This giant mural marked the first time the now-famous picture of Che by Korda was used publicly in Cuba. It was erected several stories high in the Plaza. My father took this image, one of his most famous, with the Cuban flag flying in front of the mural and a soldier standing below in the corner. Che always saw his role as exporting the Revolution—to go to Venezuela, Peru, Nicaragua, and Bolivia, to go into the bush with the guerrillas in the different Latin American countries. Che always wanted to get training, to get ready and prepare for another revolution. Cuba was always a transitory thing for him. It was always on the table that he was going to go someday. Fidel always agreed with that. Che's dream was that one day he was going to go to Argentina for a revolution. Of course, he never got the chance.

THE BAY OF PIGS
AND THE COLD WAR

cuba versus the free world

THE COLLAPSE OF COMMUNISM—and with it the tearing down of the Iron Curtain and its most potent symbol, the Berlin Wall—makes the Cold War an increasingly distant memory for most people. But in Cuba, the Cold War defined post-revolutionary life. ▷ Castro set Cuban-U.S. Cold War conflict in motion in May 1959, just four months after his successful revolution, by enacting the Agrarian Reform Law, which seized hundreds of thousands of acres of U.S.-owned properties. A year later, he established diplomatic relations with the Soviet Union, spurring then-President Dwight D. Eisenhower to cancel the U.S. "sugar quota" and effectively cut Cuban exports to the United States by 80 percent. ▷ The United States followed this economic blow with a full trade embargo. Cuba responded by officially aligning itself with Soviet policies at home and abroad. ▷ All these events helped steel American resolve that Castro, although he had not yet proclaimed himself a Communist, would have to go. ▷ Unquestionably the greatest disaster of the Kennedy administration was the failed Bay of Pigs invasion, in which some 1,500 Cuban exiles, trained and supplied by the U.S. government, attacked Fidel Castro's Cuba in early 1961, just three months after the Democratic president's inauguration. This ill-conceived attempt to unseat Castro also helped light the fuse on the Missile Crisis in which the Cold War between the United States and the Soviet Union reached its hottest flash point. ▷ The immediate precursor to the Bay of Pigs invasion was a surprise air strike on April 15, 1961. Eight U.S. Air Force B-26 light bombers, painted with decoy Cuban Air Force insignia, flew under CIA direction from Nicaragua to attack a main front of Cuban defense: three military air bases. Only six planes made their targets. ▷ The CIA had hoped that Cuban markings on the planes would convince the world that Castro defectors had staged the air raid—a ruse that failed miserably and provoked international protests. The bombings did succeed in destroying some of Castro's air force; however, it is a testament to the Cuban leader's skill as a tactician that with his meager remaining planes he wreaked havoc on the real invading forces two days later. ▷ That attack came soon after 1 A.M. on April 17, when the exile-commandos started landing on Playa Girón at the Bay of Pigs. Castro dispatched troops and tanks to the scene. Meanwhile, Cuba's remaining air force of five light bombers and two jet trainers armed with 50-caliber machine guns devastated the ships supplying reinforcements, ammunition, and supplies to the forces that had already landed. Part of Castro's success is attributed to President Kennedy's reluctance to send more U.S. planes down to Cuba after the embarrassing initial air strike. ▷ Whatever the reason, Castro's personally-led artillery, tanks, and militia mopped up on the stranded invaders. When the shooting was over on April 19, Castro's men had taken nearly 1,200 prisoners and had killed 114 invaders, compared to 161 Cuban deaths. ▷ The fiasco of the Bay of Pigs led directly to the Missile Crisis. After the invasion, the Soviets began supplying arms to Cuba. Kennedy's policy on the buildup was that so long as the weapons were "defensive," there would be no American intervention.   By late August 1962, however, U.S. spy planes had photographed SAM-2 missile sites on the island. The following month, Soviet troops—eventually some forty thousand strong—began to arrive in Cuba. In October, medium-range ballistic missiles and Soviet bombers appeared as well. Toward the end of the crisis, the Russians claimed that their arms buildup in Cuba was a response to the U.S. military's earlier placement of Jupiter nuclear missiles in Turkey, none of which prevented the nerve-racking standoff.   On October 22, President Kennedy shocked the American public in a television address announcing the Missile Crisis and the American blockade of Cuba. Russian Premier Nikita Khrushchev continued to claim that the Soviet missiles were defensive and vowed to send more.   The ensuing game of cat-and-mouse between the two superpowers brought the world to the brink of nuclear war.   On October 24, a U.S. naval quarantine of Cuba went into effect aimed at stopping, searching, and sending back ships bearing nuclear weapons, and U.S. Strategic Air Command nuclear bombers were ordered into condition DEFCON 2 for the first time in history, the last step before the declaration of nuclear war.   Finally, on October 28, Khrushchev announced on Radio Moscow that he was backing down. He agreed to call back Soviet freighters carrying weapons and to withdraw the missiles already in place on Cuban soil. His announcement, done without the prior knowledge of Fidel Castro, sent the Cuban leader into a cursing rage. The rest of the world breathed a sigh of relief.   The Missile Crisis did have some positive effects, however. For one, it had shaken both superpowers out of their deadly stalemate. Immediately following the event, a hot line between the White House and the Kremlin was installed to keep the countries' leaders in direct contact in times of crisis. Likewise, previously stalled U.S.-USSR talks on a "limited test-ban treaty" on nuclear weapons were reopened, inspiring the following year's ban on airborne, undersea, and outer-space testing.   Throughout the '70s and '80s, U.S. presidents protested the placement of Soviet troops and defensive armaments in Cuba, but no situation advanced anywhere near the brink that the Missile Crisis had reached.   As an interesting sidelight, in the sixteen-page letter that Khrushchev sent to Kennedy ending the Missile Crisis in 1962, he also asked that America end its economic embargo of Cuba and withdraw from its long-standing naval base at Guantánamo at the eastern end of the island.   But Khrushchev had lost his bargaining power. The two requests were ignored by Kennedy. America's embargo of Cuba and its naval base on Cuban soil remain to this day, mute but powerful testament to the continuing global fascination with a solitary man and his small island: Fidel's Cuba.

FIREMAN WITH DESTROYED PLANES

SANTIAGO DE CUBA, 1961 — In this photo, a fireman is putting out the fire in the wreckage of planes bombed in the aerial attack on Santiago de Cuba, two days before the Bay of Pigs invasion. Cuba had three main airports in those days. Near Havana there was Ciudad Libertad (Liberty City) and San Antonio de los Baños. And there was the airport at Santiago de Cuba, down in the far southeastern end of the island. The mercenary bombers tried to knock out all the Cuban Air Force simultaneously. So, they hit those three air bases. The CIA-backed bomber pilots thought they were knocking out the military planes. But in this photograph, these are all civilian DC-3s. The bombers missed most of the war planes. (Cuba lost five military planes, but eight survived to wreak havoc at the Bay of Pigs.)

CUBAN SOLDIER AT THE SIDE OF A TANK

BAY OF PIGS, 1961 — After the bombings at the airports, we knew an invasion was coming. But we didn't know where. The *Revolución* editor, Carlos Franqui, sent (photographers Alberto) Korda to Pinar del Rio; Liborio Noval went to Guantánamo; Mayito (Mario García Joya) went to Santa Clara; I was stuck in Oriente. My father and (Raúl) Corrales were in Havana as reserve. In the first hours, we still didn't know if it was the main thrust. They sent Ernesto Fernandez, a second-stringer, to the Bay of Pigs. As the story wound up, Ernesto covered the fighting. He was the only one to get pictures of the action. Mayito showed up on the 19th in the morning. Corrales got there at mid-morning. My father showed up at mid-afternoon. All these *Revolución* photographers arrived down at the Bay of Pigs against orders, because, dammit, they wanted pictures! The thing was over by 5:40 P.M. on the 19th. That's water on the side of the tank, even if it looks like blood.

BAY OF PIGS, 1961 — Fidel rushed to the Bay
of Pigs as soon as he knew that was the invasion point. He personally led the troops down
there. Actually, in Cuba, we call the invasion
"Playa Girón," after the beach on the Bay of
Pigs where the mercenaries landed.

BAY OF PIGS, 1961 — As you can see from the faces of these guys, the militiamen who fought at the Bay of Pigs were pretty young. My father shot some twenty portraits. He had plans for a book on "The Faces of the Bay of Pigs."

BAY OF PIGS, 1961

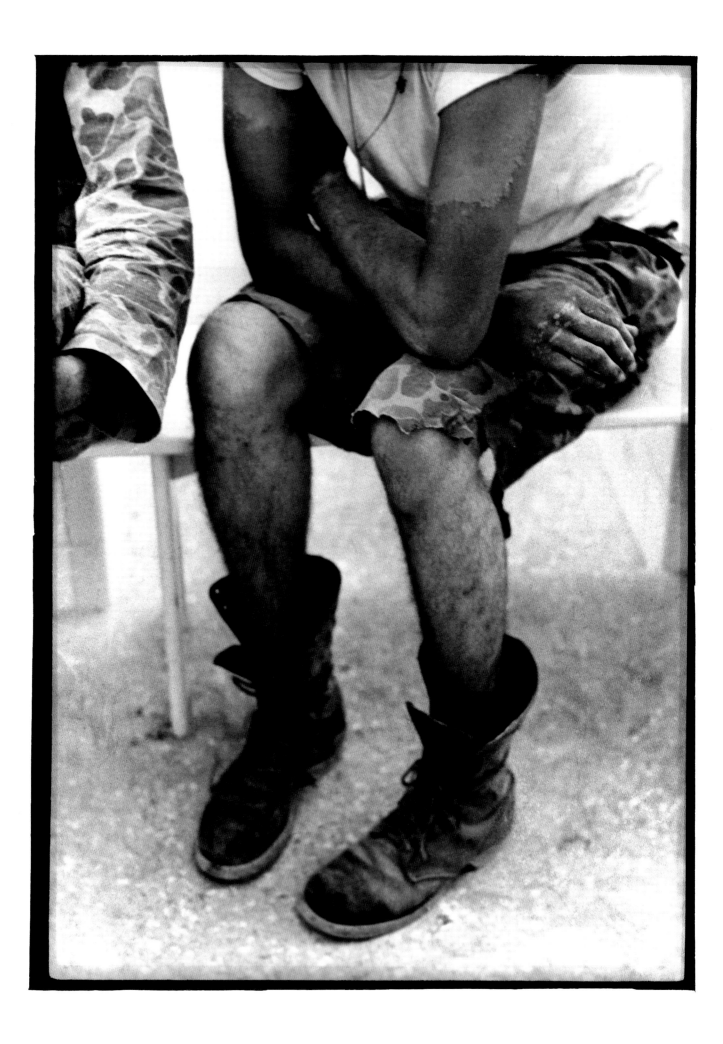

DEFEAT

BAY OF PIGS, 1961 — My old man took this picture of one of the mercenaries. You don't even need to see the guy's face. It's the picture of defeat: his muddy arm, the torn uniform, the soggy boots. The guys who landed had no idea of the opposition they were going to be up against. They had brought band uniforms and instruments with them. They thought they were just going to come into town with a marching band and the people would welcome them with open arms. The instruments and band uniforms got sunk on the ships they'd come on. The mercenaries were supposed to hold a piece of land for forty-two to seventy-two hours, declare themselves the new Cuban government, and (U.S. President John F.) Kennedy would recognize them and send in massive military support to get rid of Fidel. Right.

IN THE STUDIO WITH THE INVADERS

1961 — I took this of Fidel addressing the prisoners of war, the captured mercenaries from the Bay of Pigs. It was televised to the whole country. Fidel's interviewing them, asking them what they thought they were doing. They all had white T-shirts and green camouflage pants. You can't put it past the Company (CIA)—they outfitted them well. But the Company didn't figure on what Fidel could do.

1962 — These are some of the Bay of Pigs
POWs, getting ready to board a flight back to
the United States. Fidel put a price on each
man's head, depending on his rank. Cuba got
payment in food and medicine (worth more
than $60 million) as ransom. Fidel ransomed
more than one thousand men.

MILICIANA

1963 — This is one of the *miliciana* (female militia). After they had proved themselves in the war against Batista, Fidel was a strong supporter of women in uniform. There were quite a few of them in the early '6os, because there was a lot of paranoia about another U.S. invasion.

NICARAGUA, 1981 — After we had finished our work for *Revolución*, my father traveled frequently to other countries to take pictures for *Granma*. This was from his trip to Nicaragua, not long after they'd won their revolution against Somoza. The "FSLN" flag the little boy is holding is the official standard of the Sandanista National Liberation Front. My old man won a prize in Japan with this picture.

HAVANA, 1961 — The famous Soviet cosmonaut Yuri Gagarin, the first man in space, was visiting Cuba at the time of the 26th of July celebration in 1961. This was only a few months after the Bay of Pigs invasion. Here Fidel's giving him a big hug while President Dorticos looks on. Fidel also gave Gagarin the new Order of Girón medal. But somebody suggested that Cuba give him a more "personal" gift. I've always loved parrots, so

I said we should give him that. Somebody said, "Great, get the cosmonaut a parrot." So, me and one of the other guys looked all over Havana for a parrot. We could only find two, and they were both a mess. They looked like hell. The guy who sold them to us said they'd clean up nice. So, I took them to this hangar where they had a high-pressure hose and squirted the hell out of them to get them clean. We gave Yuri Gagarin the parrots with

a cover over their cage, and he was very grateful. He got back on his military transport to Moscow. The next time somebody from Cuba saw him, they asked, "So, how'd you like those parrots?" He said, "Those Cuban parrots are crazy! You can't go near them or they yell their heads off. They went nuts on the plane back to Russia." I guess I'd given those poor birds a complex, but I was just trying to clean them up.

HAVANA, January 1974 — This visit from
Leonid Brezhnev, the guy who took over from
Khrushchev, was a really big deal for Fidel. It
was real recognition from the Soviet Union.
It marked the first time a supreme Soviet
leader had ever come to Cuba—or anywhere
in Latin America, for that matter.

CUBA:
THE LAND AND THE PEOPLE

the faces of those who endure

THE GREAT IRONY of Cuba is that of a land blessed with natural beauty yet fraught with turmoil and bloodshed throughout its history. ▷ One year after Christopher Columbus "discovered" the island in 1492, the pope ceded Cuba to Spain with the mission of converting the more than one hundred thousand peaceful indigenous Indians to Christianity. ▷ The harsh Spanish rule gave Cuba its first revolutionary hero, the Indian chief Hatuey, who was burned at the stake in 1512 for refusing to capitulate to the European invaders. Slave trade began on the island a year later, growing rapidly more heartless and lucrative. African slaves began arriving a decade after that and would continue to do so until the late 1800s. ▷ Sixteenth-century Cuba experienced an economic boom thanks to sugar, aggressive slave trading, and visiting Spanish treasure fleets that stopped over while bound for Mother Spain with silver and gold from the Americas. But with the treasure ships came hundreds of notorious pirates led by ruthless men like Henry Morgan. Havana and other cities on the island were frequently sacked. ▷ A century of Spanish murder, forced labor, and imported diseases like smallpox effectively wiped out Cuba's indigenous peoples. These events ushered in the almost exclusively Spanish and African bloodlines that still comprise the bulk of the current population. ▷ The first great war of independence against the Spanish colonialists came in 1868, led by abolitionist plantation owner Carlos Manuel de Céspedes. That war raged for ten years and ended with an amnesty. But it did not provide the autonomy that Creole Cubans had fought for. ▷ José Martí, the great revolutionary hero in Cuban history, led the second war of independence. Coming out of exile in New York, he led an invasion in 1895 in eastern Cuba not far from the invasion point chosen by Fidel Castro, his devout follower, sixty-one years later. Martí's rebellion, on the verge of triumph, was upstaged in 1898 by the U.S. intercession and victory in the Spanish-American War. ▷ Relinquishing military control, the United States allowed Cuba to become an independent republic (at least in name) in 1902. Political strife reigned, inspiring a second U.S. invasion in 1906. Three years later, with a U.S.-approved president in power, Cuba began its long history of rule by corrupt, racially biased leaders. The United States again intervened militarily in Cuba in 1912, putting down revolt, and in 1917, to protect the sugar industry. ▷ A nearly endless wave of corrupt rulers continued with Alfonso y Zayas (1921–25) and the murderous Gerardo Machado y Morales (1925–33). Fulgencio Batista and his string of puppet presidents (1933–44) offered slight relief from corruption—his first regime being far more paternal than his last. However, presidents Ramón Grau St. Martín (1944–48) and Carlos Prío Socarrás (1948–52) devastated the Cuban economy through their greed. When a much-hardened Batista returned from his eight-year sojourn in Miami bent on milking Cuba for every peso he could steal, he set the stage for Castro's revolution. ▷ Cuba has been wracked since 1959 by numerous losses: thousands of its soldiers sent to fight in foreign wars (in Ethiopia and Angola), the devastating end to Soviet financial support, the internecine defections of countless Cubans to south Florida in the Mariel and *balsero* "boatlifts," and the stiffening of the U.S. trade embargo by the Helms-Burton Act of the mid-1990s. ▷ Castro's communist regime did introduce much-needed improvements in healthcare and education during its first four decades, but today the majority of the population remains dirt-poor; everything from food to gasoline is rationed. The Yankee dollar is once more required currency for anything beyond the most basic commodities. ▷ Yet the spirit of the Cuban people seems unbroken despite centuries of hardships. In modern Havana, children still play stickball daily along the Prado, and lovers continue to stroll nightly on the oceanfront Malecón. Music enlivens the vestibules of run-down apartment buildings, exclusive hotel verandas, and glittering salsa palaces. Excellent native rum and cigars, however hard for locals to come by, are not yet for wealthy tourists alone. ▷ On any given evening in the island's capital of two million people, one can still find far more good humor than can be had in similarly populated North American cities. Despite Cuba's seemingly endless parade of travails, whatever has inspired her people's passion for life appears to endure.

THE CUBAN LOTTERY

SANTIAGO DE CUBA, 1959 — This is a *billetero* (ticket seller) carrying his lottery board. Under Batista, the lottery was a corrupt system. The Revolution used it for some time, until it disappeared around 1962, to collect funds to build apartments. They used it to move people into Havana from the shacks they'd been living in. Some of those buildings constructed with lottery money are still standing around town.

1959 — This is just a moment from the first days of the Revolution. Recently, the Minister of Culture asked me, "Why aren't the young photographers taking pictures today in 'the Special Period' (of austerity, which began in 1990) like you used to in the '60s for *Revolución*?" I told the guy, "Look, things were happening in the '60s. Objects. People. Things were moving, man." These days, how are the young photographers supposed to show the Special Period? A guy who normally waited ten minutes at the bus stop now waits three and a half hours. How do you reflect that? With a line at a bus stop? There are lines at bus stops all over the world.

THE FAMILY

PINAR DEL RIO, 1960 — For me, this is the classic picture of a *guajiro* (peasant) family. It looks like a poster for a film about the Revolution. Pinar del Rio is the westernmost region of Cuba, and it's where the great tobacco is grown for cigars. You can see how rough the ground is there.

They used oxen to till the soil. I remember when tractors finally started to be used in the '60s, I did a pictorial feature on them for *Revolución*. I had a picture of an ox pulling a plow. The headline said, "This is a scene from the past." Well, today, with the way things are in Cuba, the oxen are back.

FARMER

PINAR DEL RIO, 1960 — This is an old Chinese farmer enjoying his pipe. There used to be a lot of Chinese in Cuba. Originally, they'd been brought to Cuba as a replacement to the slave labor, from the late 1890s to about 1915. But when the Revolution came, all the Chinese in Havana couldn't make any money with their dry-cleaning places and restaurants. They took off for Miami, New York, who knows where. We've still got a Chinatown in Havana. The restaurants are there, and there's a Chinese archway leading into that section of Old Havana. We've got a Chinatown with no Chinese.

GREGORIO "OLD MAN AND THE SEA" FUENTES

COJIMAR, 1976 — Gregorio Fuentes was nearly eighty when this picture was taken. But he still looks pretty good here. He skippered Ernest Hemingway's fishing boat, *El Pilar*, from 1938 until the writer killed himself in 1961. Fuentes likes to say he was Hemingway's model for Santiago, the fisherman in the Nobel Prize–winning novel *The Old Man and the Sea*. There are many versions of that story. During World War II, Fuentes and Papa used to patrol the Cuban coastline, looking for German U-boats. Lucky for them they never found any. Gregorio's still around; he's 101. He still smokes. And if you show up with a bottle of whiskey, you're lucky if he doesn't drink the whole thing.

1963 — These are two images from my first personal show of photographs, four years after moving to Cuba. The whole show was on Santería and Afro-Cuban religions. Young photographers are still doing photographic essays on Santería. In 1998, I had my fiftieth one-man show. It featured double exposures of cockfights and nudes.

1963 — This mother and child were victims of
Hurricane Flora, one of the biggest storms
ever to hit Cuba. It was the first time in Cuban
history that a hurricane came up and down,
back and forth. It hit the island five times. It
had practically no wind but lots of water.
More than one thousand people died.

1964 — This lady picking tomatoes was from a series I wanted to do for *Cuba* magazine. Cuba is a macho society. Men do everything. Women are supposed to stay home and give birth. I wanted to show women ten thousand miles away from maternity wards and fashion shows. This woman is a *campesina* (female farmer).

PINAR DEL RIO, 1965 — These pictures were taken while I was doing a story for *Cuba* magazine on the Matahambre copper mines in the western part of the island. It's one of the deepest copper mines in the world. It goes down some four thousand yards. These miner guys are macho, and they don't let people into their group very easily. To win their confidence, I went and asked to do volunteer work in the mines. They thought I was bullshitting them. I wanted to work for one of the meanest son-of-a-bitches there. I did full shifts from 7 A.M. to 3 P.M., four thousand yards deep, for ten or fifteen days. After that, I broke the circle. And they let me photograph them. I ruined a Leica down there in the mines. The picture below is of Lola, the telephone operator at the mine. Over her head you can see the archaic system she used for the switchboard duties. There's also a 26th of July sticker with Fidel's face on it. Lola was great. Every afternoon, I'd go over to the little shack where she took care of the switchboard, and she'd make me a coffee. We'd talk a while, and then she'd let me call my family back in Havana for free.

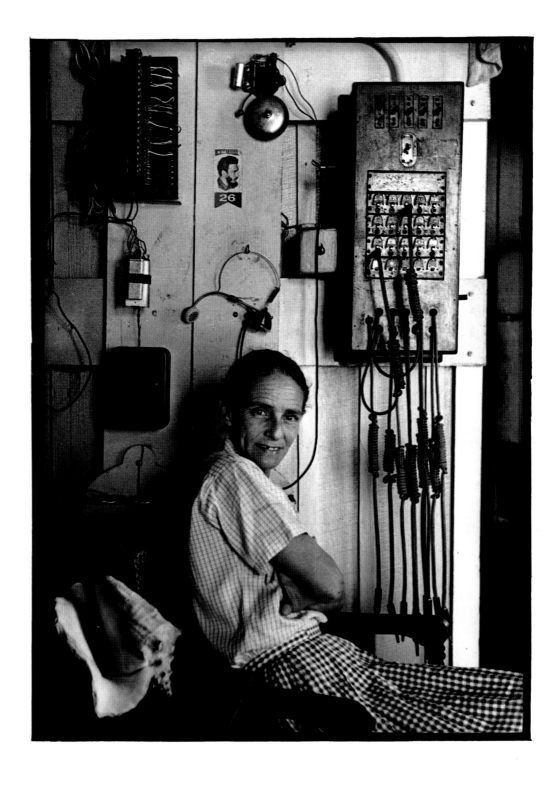

CIÉNAGA DE ZAPATA, 1965 — This fellow is a *carbonero* (charcoal maker) in the region of Zapata, near the Bay of Pigs. That place is famous for its charcoal. They made charcoal by putting it in these huge stacks, covering it with dirt, and letting it burn from the inside out. It doesn't get any air that way and turns into charcoal. The *campesinos* use it for cooking in their homes.

HERMANOS

SANTA CLARA, July 1966 — These guys from the mid-'60s still reflect Cuba today: the Spanish and the black descendants, standing side by side. My father named the photo "Hermanos" (brothers), because racial prejudice is pretty much nonexistent in Cuba. It's more elastic here than in the States.

CANE CUTTERS

1970 — This is from my series on Cuban workers. They're still cutting sugarcane at sundown. Somebody recently complimented this shot as "artistic." But I don't call it art. When somebody says to me, "I'm an art photographer," I say, "Oh, really? You photograph the paintings in a museum?" I think there's too many people blowing photographers up like balloons. Me? I'm just a photographer. If somebody considers what I do as art—that's great.

1966 — This picture shows several genera-
tions of progress, from horse-drawn labor,
to the train, to the automobile in the background. My father captured it pretty
effectively. That's Cuba: it's pretty rural.
After we'd been back in Cuba for many
years, my father said to me one day, "Maybe
I did the wrong thing bringing you back. You
could have stayed in New York." See, he
never appreciated that his father took him
out of Cuba. So, the old man was worried
that maybe he did the wrong thing pushing
me to move here. I said, "Look, Pop.
I wanted to come here. It was my choice."

MAN AND MACHETE

1968 — This picture is of a cane cutter, a *machetero*, at the end of the work day. Cutting sugarcane's the toughest job in the world. It's hot and brutal. You get cut up pretty good by those sharp shoots of cane after you chop it. This picture of my father's reminds me of his shot of Che, squatting down and laughing with his muddy boots on, at the end of one of his work days.

LANGOSTINO

ISLE OF PINES, 1970 — This is also from my
worker series. It's a *langostino* (saltwater
prawn) fisherman as seen from above.
I liked the angle.

1971 — After years of working in the fields, you can see the cane cutter's back (on the right) has turned into that certain bend that they all get. Even in profile, in silhouette, he's got that certain bent back. You can tell him right away. He's a professional. He grew up doing that. He's a cane cutter.

NIGHT CARNIVAL

HAVANA, circa 1980 — This is a shot of the night carnival in Havana. It was sort of like Mardi Gras. They used to hold carnival in February. They spent a lot of time building floats and clothes, and it was great because, at that time of year, there was never any rain. Then they moved the carnival to the 26th of July—the Revolution Carnival—and everybody got rained on big time. In Brazil, they're crazy with the carnivals. They measure the success by how many people get killed during carnival. A lot of dead: a good carnival. But in Havana, it was pretty controlled. Three blocks away you didn't know they were having a carnival. Since "the Special Period": no carnival.

SOMBREROS

1975 — I like this one because you've got all those hats of the *guajiros* (farmers), and that one dress hat, right up front, in the same crowd.

THREE GENERATIONS

1996 — This is a recent one. The Chinese gave
me a prize for it. It's a grandmother, mother,
and baby. I wanted to do an updated photographic story on birth since I'd done one for
Cuba magazine back in the '6os.

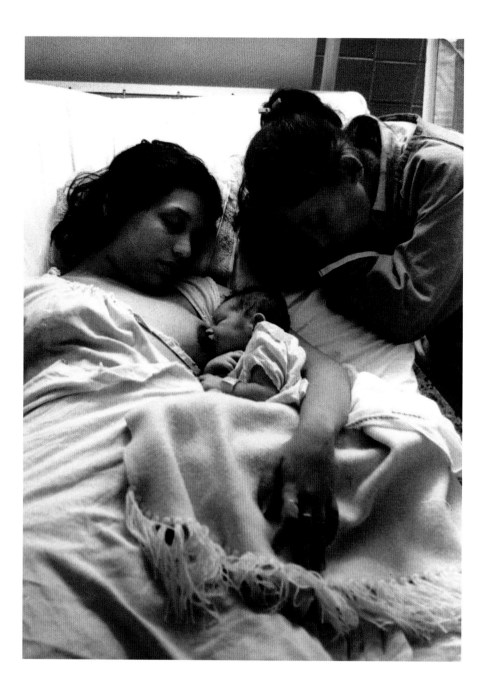

1977 — The fellow in this picture is one hundred years old. My father was sixty-three when he took it. I've always tried to follow my father's advice. He said, "The best photograph you've taken is the one you'll take tomorrow." That's what keeps me shooting.

a cuban chronology

3500 B.C.
The first indigenous people (cave dwellers) arrive in Cuba from South America.

1492
Explorer Christopher Columbus lands in Cuba, declaring it the most beautiful spot on earth.

1493
The pope gives Spain control of Cuba and the mission of converting its native population to Christianity.

1512
The first Spanish town is founded at Baracoa by Velásquez.

The Indian leader Hatuey leads the island's first battle of independence against the Spanish; he is burned at the stake.

1513
The first slaves are shipped to Cuba.

1515
Santiago de Cuba becomes the island's capital.

1518
The explorer Hernándo Cortéz makes the first of his notorious trips from Cuba to Mexico in search of gold.

1519
The city of Havana is established.

1521
Ponce de León, who discovered Florida—and searched in vain for the fabled "Fountain of Youth"—dies in Cuba.

1536
The first of decades-long pirate attacks are launched against Havana.

1548
Sugarcane becomes a commercial crop for the first time.

1558
Havana becomes the official capital.

1580
Cuba's world-famous tobacco industry begins in earnest.

1586
English sea legend Sir Francis Drake makes an unsuccessful attack on Cuba.

1662
Famed British sailor Captain Henry Morgan begins his series of attacks on Cuban port towns.

1700s
Tobacco becomes the main export.

1728
The University of Havana is founded.

1762
The British invade Cuba, occupying Havana for a year.

1800
There are now some 500,000 slaves on the island.

1808
Thomas Jefferson tries unsuccessfully to buy Cuba for the United States.

1837
A railroad is constructed from Havana to Bejucal.

1844
H. Upmann opens its celebrated cigar factory in Havana.

1848
U.S. President James Polk attempts unsuccessfully to buy Cuba.

1850
Four hundred American troops land in Cuba and are defeated by the Spanish in an eerie parallel to the disastrous Bay of Pigs incident a century later.

1853
José Martí, Cuba's most famous patriot, is born.

1854
U.S. President Franklin Pierce attempts unsuccessfully to buy Cuba from the Spanish.

1868
Slavery is abolished.

1868–78
The first war of independence from Spanish control is led by Carlos Manuel de Céspedes.

1887
José Martí comes to live in the United States to raise money and organize a revolutionary party bent on liberating Cuba.

1895–98
The second war of independence is led by José Martí, who is killed early in the fighting.

1898
The U.S. battleship *The Maine* mysteriously blows up in Havana harbor.

The Spanish-American War is declared by Congress; Teddy Roosevelt and the Rough Riders become heroes for Americans at home.

Spanish rule finally ends in Cuba.

1901
The Platt Amendment is imposed on Cuba, a false independence based on decades of American intervention to come.

1902
Cuba achieves independence.

1903
The United States establishes a naval base at Guantánamo Bay.

1906
U.S. military intervention puts down an insurrection; the United States establishes a temporary provisional government on the island.

1912
The U.S. military intercedes in the "Negro insurrection" led by Evaristo Estenoz, hero of the war of independence.

1917
President Woodrow Wilson sends U.S. troops to Cuba to quell a Liberal Party uprising.

1925
The disastrous presidency of Gerardo Machado begins.

The first Communist Party is founded.

1926
Fidel Castro is born in Oriente province.

1933
The Machado dictatorship is overthrown; Fulgencio Batista begins his first reign.

1934
The Platt Amendment is abrogated by U.S. President Franklin Roosevelt.

1944
Cuban President Fulgencio Batista loses his bid for reelection and flees to exile in Florida, taking with him an estimated $20 million in spoils.

1952
Fulgencio Batista comes out of retirement to regain control of Cuba by military coup.

1953
Fidel Castro makes his disastrous July 26th attack on the Moncada barracks.

1955
Castro is released from prison and goes into self-imposed exile in Mexico.

1956
Castro's freedom fighters sail from Mexico to Cuba to begin their revolution.

1958
Che Guevara captures Santa Clara.

1959
Batista flees to the Dominican Republic; Castro's revolution prevails.

1959–65
The period of epic revolutionary photography begins at the newspaper *Revolución*.

1960
Large companies are nationalized in a move against what Castro calls "U.S. economic aggression."

The U.S. economic embargo begins.

Castro visits the United Nations in New York City and speaks for four hours, criticizing U.S. monopolists and imperialists.

1961
The Bay of Pigs invasion fails.

Castro makes Cuba officially socialist, aligning his nation with the Soviet Union.

1962
U.S. President John F. Kennedy orders a total trade ban with Cuba, depriving Castro's government of $35 million in annual income.

The Cuban Missile Crisis threatens world peace for seven days.

1963
The second agrarian reform law is enacted.

1967
Che Guevara is killed in Bolivia along with six others.

1975
The first Cuban Communist Party congress is held.

Cuban troops are sent to Angola.

1980
The Mariel "boatlift" carries 120,000 Cubans to Miami.

1983
Cuban workers are killed in fighting with U.S. soldiers in Grenada.

1988
Cuban troops are withdrawn from Angola.

1989
Angolan war hero General Ochoa Sánchez is executed for alleged drug dealing, shocking the nation.

1990
The collapse of the Soviet Union deprives Cuba of $5 billion in annual subsidies; Castro declares "the Special Period" of economic austerity.

1992
The Cuban Democracy Act punishes overseas subsidiaries of U.S. companies that trade with Cuba, further strengthening the trade embargo.

1993
Foreign currencies are "decriminalized" by Castro; Cubans are again allowed to trade in *Yanqui* dollars.

1994
A mass exodus of more than 30,000 Cubans fails and the "rafters" are turned back from the United States to land at Guantánamo Naval Base.

1995
Castro allows small businesses to operate— including produce markets and independent restaurants.

1996
The United States tightens its economic blockade of Cuba with the Helms-Burton Act.

Two private planes piloted by Miami-based Cuban exiles on a "rescue" mission to the island are shot down by the Cuban Air Force.

1997
The Cuban population is eleven million.

Castro allows Cubans to celebrate Christmas again, for one year only, in preparation for a visit by the pope.

1998
Pope John Paul II makes an unprecedented visit to Cuba, to the delight of native Catholics and the Western news media, who flock to the island by the thousands.

The Cuban government criticizes a U.S. initiative to send humanitarian aid to Cuba while maintaining the thirty-six-year-old economic embargo.